# ESSAYS ON PRIMORDIAL RELIGION

**GANGMUMEI KAMEI**

*Former Minister,*
*Higher Education, Environment and Law ,*
*Government of Manipur*

**AKANSHA PUBLISHING HOUSE**
**NEW DELHI**

**AKANSHA PUBLISHING HOUSE**
4649-B/21, Ansari Road
Darya Ganj
New Delhi - 110 002
Ph. : 23263193 / 9811582579
Email: ektabooks@yahoo.com

**Essays on Primordial Religion**



Reprint 2026

ISBN 81-8370-049-7



PRINTED IN INDIA

---

Published by M.P. Misra for Akansha Publishing House, New Delhi and Printed at Tarun Offset Press, Delhi.

Dedicated

to

SHRI MARULUNG REMMEI, MSS (Retd)

Writer, Administrator and Religious leader

# PREFACE

There has been recently a renewed interest on the religion of the tribal people in the wake of the global movement for the assertion of the indigenous people. In India, there is introspection among the elite of the tribal communities to assert and preserve their culture and religion on the onslaught of the proselytizing world religions. The religion of the tribal community is being sidelined by the alien religions. This small compendium of four lectures delivered by me on different occasions shows the attempt made by the community and religious leaders for the preservation and revitalization of their indigenous faiths. It is an humble attempt to define the indigenous faiths of the tribal people.

The first essay "The Primordial Religion: Defining the Tribal religion" was read at the National Seminar on Indigenous Religions of North east India, organized by the Centre for Study of Civilizations, New Delhi. Primordial Religion: A case study of Zeliangrong religion was read at a Study Circle at Manipur University in 1992 and published in the International Anthropological Journal of Indian Anthropological Society through the courtesy of Prof. A.K. Danda of Asiatic society, Calcutta. It has been improved upon from the original text. The original title was the Philosophy and Theology of the Zeliangrong Religion. The indigenous Faiths Reform Movements in North East India was a paper entitled Revitalization of indigenous Faiths presented to the National Seminar on the Comparative Study of Religions of North East India, sponsored by the Indian Institute of Advanced Studies, Shimla and organized by the Department of Philosophy, Manipur University, Canchipur, Imphal 26th - 29th June 2004 and published with the permission of Prof. S. lokendrajit Singh, Professor of Philosophy, Manipur University. I have added a chapter on "Four Indigenous Faiths of other lands."

I understand that the subject requires a deeper and intensive treatment. However, this small work is being published in the growing interest of the educated people who follow their own religion and feel proud of their faith and culture. I hope there will be a better understanding of the tribal indigenous faith.

I am grateful to my friend Shri Jagdamba Mall of Kohima for encouraging me to publish this small work. I thank Mrs. Kavi Raleng, Principal, DAV Public School, Imphal for her help and encouragement in writing this book. I thank Shri Bharat Kumarji of Heritage Foundation, Guwahati, for sending me the literatures on Seng Khasi and other related papers. I thank Shri Ch. Radheyshyam, Librarian of Manipur University for giving me access to his library. I am thankful to Shri A. kamson for sending me the photos of the Maori myth. I also thank Professor N. Joykumar Singh, Director of Centre for Manipur Studies of Manipur University for going through the manuscripts and encouragement.

I thank Shri M.P. Misra, the proprietor of Akansha Publishing House, New Delhi for publishing the small work.

21st October 2005 **GANGMUMEI KAMEI**

# CONTENTS

## CHAPTER ONE

# THE PRIMORDIAL RELIGION: DEFINING THE TRIBAL RELIGION

Man is a thinking and speaking being who always believes in the supernatural as the cause, continuity and end of his existence. There are no people without a religion. Religion is the system of worship of God by men with a code of moral, spiritual and social behaviour in dealing with God and society. The indigenous people have a religion of their own for ages. Religion has been the core of the indigenous way of life. Their religion has been misinterpreted by the anthropologists, Christian missionaries and scholars of comparative theology as "animism".

### TYLOR'S ANIMISM

Sir Edward B. Tylor (1832-1917) who is generally accepted as the father of social anthropology was the first scholar who propounded the concept of animism in his paper entitled, "Religion of Savages" in the Fortnightly Review (1866) in which he wrote, "The theory which endows the phenomenon of nature with personal life might perhaps conveniently be called 'animism'." He further developed it in greater detail in his classic, Primitive Culture: Researches into Development of Mythology, Philosophy, Religion, Arts and Culture" (1871). With this work, the term "animism" has stuck to Tylor's name. He further replied to the criticism of animism by his contemporaries in his paper, "On the Limits of Savage Religion" in the Journal of Anthropological Institute (1896).

Tylor describes animism as the minimal definition of the religion of the savage as "the Belief in the Spiritual Beings". Tylor's use of the term, "Savage" to mean the primitive people is a subject of critical comments. But many writers in the $19^{th}$ century Europe used this term universally. It is said that Taylor would have preferred the term "Spiritualism" to describe the primitive religion but for his dislike for a group known as the Spiritualists in the mid nineteenth century who were a religious group which had the object of establishing communication with the dead. The spiritualists sought to communicate with the dead and they were condemned by the mainstream churches.

Tylor's use of the term, animism has been described by the critics as misleading. Animism is a belief that all natural objects have souls. But his animism is more a spiritism, dealing with an unempirical world of the spirits. There had been criticism of this concept by sociologists like Andrew Lang. Emile Durkheim, R.R. Marrett and Wilhelm Schmidt as the "Belief in Spiritual Beings (Soul, ghost, demon and ghosts) did not cover the primitive religion or the religious beliefs of the tribals.

Tylor defended that his concept was an answer to the question, "What is the most rudimentary form of religion which may yet bear that name?" Tylor thought that religion was present in all cultures properly observed and it might turn out to be present everywhere. He entertained the idea of a pre-religious stage in the evolution of cultures and believed that a tribe in that stage might be found. To proceed in as systematic study of the problem, he required a minimum of religion and found it in the "Belief in the Spiritual Beings".

According to this concept, religion had evolved from a doctrine of souls arising from the spontaneous reflection upon "death, dream, apparitions to a wider doctrine of spirits" which eventually expanded to embrace "powerful demons and gods". He left out the religions of vision and passion.

Andrew Lang (1844-1912), a Scottish folklorist theorized that the primitive tribes believed in a High God, a creator of the universe and often a legislator of a moral order as found among the tribes who had been explored both by the Christian missionaries and anthropologists. Andrew Lang was pleading for the existence of a "primordial monotheism", a belief in a Supreme God among the tribes. E.B.Tylor dismissed this as an imagination of the Christian missionaries. This is not so, the concept exists in the present times among the tribes.

Wilhelm Schmidt in his "Origin of the Idea of God (1912) discovered a High God among the primitive religion and confirmed Andrew Lang's primordial monotheism. He wrote, "Tribes have a memory of a High God, a benign creator, a Father-God who is no longer worshipped because that God is not feared." Monotheism has been suggested to be more naturally primitive as a world view than animism.

It has been asserted that the tribes are found not to be animistic, as their system of religious beliefs and mode of worship of the God do not present a picture of degenerated religious practice. It has been suggested that due to the loss of contact with prophets and religious seers, they had degenerated to polytheism, worship of many gods. James Frazer in his "The Golden Bough" observed that when definite deities with specific names and functions were recognised, the animinst had become a polytheist and the term animism was no longer strictly applicable, Frazer's thesis is that animism is a stage in the evolutionary development of a tribal religion. If animism means Belief in Spiritual Beings, every religion has these rudimentary ideas in one form or the other.

In India, under the great influence of E.B. Tylor, the official administrators including ethnographers were instructed by the then British Government of India to use the term "animism" to describe the religion of the tribal or indigenous communities. They were also directed to use the term in the Census of India since 1901. In the north east, the Government of Assam published anthropological monographs from1906 onwards, like the Khasis by P.T.R. Gurdon, The Garos by A. Mayflair, The Meitheis by T.C. Hodson, The Kacharis by Rev.S. Endle, The Naga Tribes of Manipur by T.C. Hodson, The Lushai Kuki Clans by John Shakespeare, The Sema Nagas by J.H. Hutton, The Angami Nagas by J.H. Hutton, The Ao Nagas by J.P. Mills, The Lohtas Naga by J.P. Mills , The Thadou-Kukis by William Shaw, The Lushai Crysalis by A.G. McCall, The Lakhers by P.N. Perry. These powerful writings have described the tribal religion as animism. Even, the religion of the Meitheis has been wrongly described as animistic by T.C. Hodson.

Following these anthropological writers, the Christian missionaries in their declared objective of converting the tribes into Christianity had condemned the tribal religion as heathen, pagan and animistic. Their religion was described as worship of demons and evil spirits.

The tribal educated elite including the new Christian converts condemned their own religion as animism. However, enlightened scholars of the tribal communities who are the followers of the traditional religion refuse to accept the derogatory name. Even Christian writers who have sympathy for the tribal culture do not accept the appendage.

## PRIMAL RELIGION

Dr. Harold Turner, a Presbyterian theologian of New Zealand in a recent article in "A Lion Handbook: The World Religions" (1994 London) came out in a strong defence of the religion of the indigenous people. He writes, "Most of the common terms for these religions are either offensive or inaccurate. Tribal people do not like to be called heathen, savage, primitive or superstitious and words such as animistic, pre-literate, traditional or ethnic are not accurate." He pleaded that "Religion must be carefully distinguished from magic where people try to use spirit power for their selfish ends. The term "Primal Religion" has been proposed to replace Animism."

According to Turner, the word, 'Primal Religion' means the religions that are prior to the universal religions. Primal religions are not religions for all people. They are the religions of one tribe or a people who realize that other people have their own gods and religious system, the word "primal" means primary or basic. Primal religions usually have the main basic features that belong to all religions.

## TENETS OF PRIMAL RELIGIONS

Basic to primal religion is a belief in a spiritual world of power or beings stronger than man himself. Men are not alone in the universe; behind every ordinary thing and daily event there is a "spirit power" which is called Mana by the Polynesian in south Pacific, Mutunga by the South Africans and Orenda by North American Indians.

i) Every primal religion has a group of spirit power whom they call gods.

ii) Primal religions have a belief in a Supreme God above all other power. This God is thought of as a Universal God for all people (like the Great Spirit of the North American Eskimos or Indian, Io of the Maoris of New Zealand). This is the creator of all, High God, Sky God and is concerned with the moral lives of the people or community. He is the Almighty God.

iii) Ancestor Worship: Worship or Honour of the Living Dead. There is a strong belief in the continuing presence of the ancestors who are honoured rather than worshipped and remembered as human beings and not as gods.

iv) Dream and Vision:

To them myths are not fairy tales, but long and complicated stories containing people's theology and philosophy of life. Dream and vision are interpreted accordingly.

v) Rituals and Festivals: the followers of the primal religions made prayers and offerings to God or specific gods in form of sacrifice of animals, and inanimate objects like water, flower, grass, ginger, leaf etc.

vi) Medicine Men:

There are medicine men who are priest, medium, diviner, healer and shaman, but not witch doctor, sorcerer or magician. The priests perform the rituals and organise the festivals.

Dr. Turner has commented that many primal religions have collapsed under pressure in the developing areas of the world due to the Christian missionary movements, others have persisted remarkably and have adapted to change. He said, "They should never be regarded as the childish religions of the primitive people or the crazy antics of the savage dominated by the witch doctor. There are serious efforts by adult people to create and preserve a spiritual system which can sustain them both in life and death."

Turner's primal religions may fit well to the indigenous faiths of the north east India. Animism is an inaccurate and fallacious name for the religion of the indigenous people.

## THE PRIMORDIAL RELIGION

The primal religion covers all the features of the indigenous faith or the tribal religion. An indigenous faith implies an ancient root and cultural heritage, the present consciousness and future continuance. The term, "prior to the universal religion" expresses the ancient but do not necessarily represent the present status and the future. Many Indian scholars and Hindu philosophers have described Hinduism as "Sanatan Dharma" which has been interpreted as an ancient and eternal religion or way of life. Likewise applying the criteria of antiquity and eternity, the indigenous tribal religion has been also been described as Sanatan Dharma, not in the sense of Hinduism but on the basis of similarity of the tribal religion with Hinduism.

We find the similarity in essence to indigenous faith with some popular form of Hinduism. Therefore, it is thought that the more appropriate term to describe the indigenous tribal faith is "Primordial religion" meaning a religion with a primordial existence; existing since the beginning of time. Primordiality is basic to any religion which is based on a myth of creation which ascribes to the Supreme Being as the Creator of the Universe, men and all living beings. I var Lissner, a German scholar in his "Man, God and Magic "used the term "primordial religion" to describe the religious beliefs of the polar tribes in a different context (Lissner : 1961;21) On the empirical level, an overview of the indigenous religions of the major tribal communities of north east India shows that they have a common feature of polytheism with a strong belief in the Supreme God, the creator and the Almighty God. These tenets meet all the essentialities of a functional religion with a philosophy and theology. The primordial religious system has the following features.

1. Belief in the Supreme God who is the creator of the Universe, benevolent and protector of men.

2. Belief in the existence of many gods and deities who are to look after the different aspects of the world, nature and the humans.
3. The concept of Ancestor worship and belief in the rebirth of soul.
4. Belief in the Heaven, the abode of God and gods; land of the Dead where the man or his soul goes after death.
5. Belief in the deities presiding over villages and places.
6. Offerings made to gods and deities in the worship or propitiation to them.
7. The performance of the Rites of Passage:

   Festivals of the community, individual ceremonies.
8. Organisation of the religion at the village levels.
9. Concept of sin as a deviation from social and moral code and customs, and retribution by God, society and man for the sin.
10. Belief in the redemption and salvation of Soul for the good doers.
11. Traditionally, the tribal religions have no founders; they are historically evolved. They do not usually have any name.

The recent trend in the primordial religion is the establishment of religious organisations which supervise their ancient religion. They have coined name or discovered ancient name for their religion. The village level religion has been upgraded to community level. They have written down the religious teachings and tenets in books in their own dialects. There is a concurrent development of religion and culture. Religion is seen as an aspect of cultural heritage and social solidarity. Leaders of the religion have developed philosophy and theology in their own way.

They give strong emphasis that primordial religion and culture are inseparable. Culture can be preserved when the religion of the community survives. There is a universal realization of the identity of the indigenous people who are aroused to fight for the preservation of their religion and culture.

## CHAPTER TWO

# FOUR INDIGENOUS FAITHS OF OTHER LANDS

The indigenous faiths, whatever name they use, are still followed or survived in different countries of the world. The indigenous people were converted into world religions in different periods of history, Hinduism, Buddhism, Christianity and Islam. In the modern times with the colonial expansion, the Christianity was spread among tribal peoples of America, Asia, Africa and the Oceania. Christian missionary activity was a tool of the colonial expansion, a vehicle through which European civilization and cultural ethos was transmitted to the indigenous colonial people. It is however among the Christian Polynesian or American Indian (Amerindian) or the African tribes that there is a revival of their traditional religion and culture which had been scorned and condemned by the Christian missionaries. Ethnicity is the primordial consciousness of the community of their root and identity. Now the aroused people are looking to their roots, their past, their culture, religion and tradition for their cultural identity. Study of the traditional tribal religion is a search for the ethnic identity of the indigenous people. The religious beliefs of indigenous communities, namely, the Polynesian Maori of New Zealand, the Zulu of South Africa, the Cherokee of the United States and the traditional cult of Sinkyo of Korea are being described in this chapter. It is a very brief reference; however, it may give a dimension to the study of indigenous faiths in our country.

## 1. THE MAORIS OF NEW ZEALAND:

The Maori is a Polynesian people. They form a part of the great Polynesian who inhabit in the South Pacific. The Maoris migrated to the present habitat, Maoriland in New Zealand, in different waves, according to their oral history, from the middle of the $12^{th}$ century to the $14^{th}$ century, from a mythical place known as Hawaiki. Archaeological excavations however indicate the evidences of the human habitation in the $9^{th}$ century AD. Hawaiki, the original homeland of the Maori is identified with Tahiti in the south Pacific.

It was the British explorer, Captain James Cook who first circumscribed the two islands of New Zealand which constituted the Maoriland in 1769-70 and wrote about the intelligence of the Maori people and the suitability of New Zealand for European colonization. The British took control of New Zealand in 1840. There was a strong resistance of the Maori against the British occupation, but in 1872, the Maoris were pacified and brought under the political system of New Zealand.

The Maori language belongs to the Eastern Polynesian sub-group of the Eastern Austronesian (Oceania) language. In 1897, the Maori language was described as one of the official languages of New Zealand. Since the middle of the nineteenth century, there was a process of social integration and acculturation amongst the Maoris and the Europeans. Generally, the Maori men married the European women. There was also a similar process of urbanization in the Maoriland. And the mixed marriages added to the wide scale mixed ancestry among the Maori.

The Maori is divided into tribes which are called Tiwi who recognised a common ancestry and having a common allegiance to a chief of clans known an ariki. Each tribe is subdivided into sub-tribe or the clan (Hapuu). The Hapuu is an important social unit which is also the primary land holding group and within whom the marriage is contracted; and they constituted an extended family or lineage (whaa nau).

The Maoris are highly conscious of the cultural domination by the whitemen through their administrative power, economic exploitation and Christian conversion. The Maori always tried to preserve their culture and identity. Maori identity means cultural identity. Being a Maori means recognising and venerating the Maori ancestors with a claim to the family land and enjoying the right to be recognised and respected as people or sons of the Maoriland. Maori identity means the community membership and shared recognition with Maori way of thinking and behaviour.

In New Zealand, the Maoris insist on the recognition and practice of the Maori cultural norms, use of Maori oratory in formal functions, action songs, formal reception to the visitors, pressing together of the noses on greeting each other, cooking over the earth ovens. The Maori carved houses are the centres of meeting and ceremony.

### *Religious Beliefs: the Concept of "Mana":*

The Maoris have common religious beliefs with other Polynesian peoples, like common Polynesian concept of "Mana". Mana is a Polynesian word meaning the supernatural power. The term has been used as an anthropological term for the power of God amongst the tribal people. According to the Maori belief Mana is the dynamic power for good and evil. This power is transmitted, controlled and encountered. The religious and magical rituals depend on the use of Mana. Mana may be activated by the ritual. Good health, fertility, security, good harvest and trade depend on the right use of Mana. Its misuse is dangerous and is a taboo to the people.

### *The Supreme God "IO":*

The Maori concept of the Supreme God is reflected in their belief on 'Io' who is the ultimate source of the supernatural power which has been described above as "Mana". This has become philosophically accepted term for supreme power or the Supreme God.

'Io' lives in the highest of the twelve heavens and exercises the ultimate control of all events. He is the supreme arbiter of gods, men and animals. Io is however known only to the carefully chosen priests and diviners. He is worshipped in isolated places where the priests and diviners offer or perform suitable rituals.

### *The Creation Myth:*

Io appears to have no connection with the actual work of creation. According to Maori myth, the primeval parents were Ranginui (father) and Papa tuanuki (mother). They were licked in an embrace; sons were born but they were kept in between them. The sons struggled to escape from the embrace of the parents, Rangi and Papa.

After the separation from his wife, Rangi became the sky and Papa became the earth. This is the beginning of the Maori concept of the sky father and earth mother. The falling rains and the rising mists are the tears of the grief of separation between the sky god and earth goddess.

### *Pantheon of Six Brother-Gods:*

The separation from their parents was followed by a fight among the brothers for power. After their fight, they were liberated into the world of light (Te Aumaerma). The six brothers became immortal gods. Each was given the headship of the departments or aspects of nature and life.

i) Tane, the leader of the brothers became the god of forest.

ii) Tangoroa became the god of seas.

iii) Tumatauenga became the god of war.

iv) Rongo was made the god of agriculture.

v) Whiro, another brother became the evil one, the ruler of darkness.

vi) Tawhurimata who stayed with his father, the Sky-god became the god of winds.

The six brothers are called power (Aura) or gods. They created a female out of the earth, and Tane breathed into it the life giving force; and the woman entered the world. She was named Heriuilitama. Tane took her as his wife. Their offspring became the human race.

***Maori Cycle of Time:***

It is said the ancient Maori thinkers thought about the beginning of time and recorded their ideas in a traditional Maori myth. The time passed through stages as given below.

i) The Time of Nothingness (Te Kore)

ii) The Time of Potential Being (Te Kore Kore)

iii) The Time of Deep Darkness (Te Poe)

The darkness was defeated and the time of light appeared into the world.

iv) The World of Light (Te Aumarama)

From the four stages or cycles of time emerged the three tier-universe.

i) The Sky (Te Rangi)

ii) The World of Light (Te Aumarema)

iii) The Great Darkness

### *The realm of the dead (Te Poe)*

Apart from these gods, there are tribal and territory gods, the family and ancestral gods, guardian deities or presiding deities of places.

The Maoris, therefore m, believe in a parallel world of gods and deities which are described by the anthropologist as spirit, so spirit world. The gods and deities are both good and bad; the bad ones like the mythical monster are to be avoided as Tapu (prohibition). The ancestor spirits who died without formal ritual being performed and the souls of the aborted foetuses give troubles to the family.

### *Life Force of Spiritual Power:*

The Maoris believe in life force which may be equated with soul. If some one's life force also known as Maori is destroyed, his spiritual power will be lost and he will die soon. Therefore, the Maoris believe:

i) The spiritual power is a gift from God. It determines the status and authority of the person concerned.

ii) Tapu is the system of prohibition, warning of danger and protecting individuals from uncontrolled spiritual power.

iii) Noa is being free from the Tapu prohibition. If a tapu is breached the danger could be cancelled by a purification ritual (Whekanus)

### *Priests and Rituals:*

The Maoris use the services of the priests in the worship of the gods and in the performance of the appropriate rituals. The priests offer ritual sat the secluded places well known for the particular deity. There is no temple or altar.

In the Maori religion, there is no sacrifice except food offerings to pacify the gods or spirits or the first fruits or crops of harvest to Rongo, the god of agriculture The heart of the first victim of a war was offered to the god of war, Tuma tuenga. Sometimes, if the victim was a man of status, the meat was eaten by the victor to gain spiritual power. This was condemned as cannibalism. The Maoris are normally not cannibals. A slave was buried below the main pole of the carved meeting house, the ceremonial house.

The priests offer ritual to the deities. So the correct recital of the hymn, known as Karakia is important. In the rituals, items of offering are mostly cooked food, water and fire to defeat the evil.

### *Dreams and Vision:*

To the Maoris, the dreams and vision are regarded as the message from the world of gods. They are explained by the priests and dream diviners. And to ward off evils, appropriate rituals are performed on behalf of the members of this family.

### *Birth and Death:*

Birth and death are important rites in Maori religion. The birth was celebrated with a feast. The father or the priest recites the hymn to have the supernatural power given to the child. There is no rite of initiation as the child is considered as a full member of the tribe from birth.

Death is lamented. And the death rituals are long and elaborate. The dead body was taken to the meeting house and kept in state for days and nights. Members of the lineage or the extended are gathered in funeral. Death ceremony is believed to be a time to express grief to say farewell to the dead, to make final reconciliation and to send the dead person's soul to the ancient homeland (Hawaiki), where he will live with his ancestors. The mourning is public and the rites are carried out at the meeting house, for the deceased, according to Maori belief, belongs to the tribe and not to the individual family.

### *Land of the Dead:*

The Maori have a concept of the land of the dead where the soul of the dead goes after death. They live a life similar to that of the human world. The land of dead is guarded by the Great Hino of the Dark through whom all the dead to reach the underworld. The female goddess of the land of the dead was originally the wife of Tane who later on fled from her husband.

## 2. THE ZULUS OF SOUTH AFRICA:

Dr. Anel-Iva Bergland of Upsala University of Sweden writing on the Zulu religion of South Africa observes, "Recent studies on African traditional beliefs have shown quite convincingly that African ideas and religious convictions are not primitive in an evolutionistic sense. Nor are they backward and without sense. Quite the contrary, thought and belief expressed in ritual and in life attitudes make sense and one fully logically, if they are seen from the angles of those who live these thought pattern."

According to him, "Zulus are a good illustration of how an African traditional religion can adapt and accommodate itself to new ideas and symbols."

### *The African Religions:*

According to Newell S. Booth Jr., the African religion including the Zulu religion have some commonality which is universal among the religions of the tribes and communities in Africa.

i) The African religion is traditional, handed down orally from generation to generation. The word of the elder through whom the tradition is transmitted is regarded as final. An African community consists of those who share a common tradition. In African religion, the community is of the highest value. The individual exists for the community; and to be cut off from the community is worse than death.

ii) Birth is a process of becoming human. The African religion focuses on the human beings rather than the supernatural phenomena or beings. They aim at enhancing the human value in the community. Birth is only the beginning of becoming a human being. A child must have first a name, usually an ancestral name.

iii) Initiation is the first stage of separation from the mother and the female world.

iv) Marriage takes place after a man is initiated. There is no marriage without initiation. Marriage of an uninitiated is an outrage. Marriage is a community affair. It is not the individuals but the families who marry. To have children is the most important duty of a man. A person without a child cannot become an ancestor and he does not participate in the continuity of community life.

v) Death: Life ends in death. Death is inevitable but it is not welcomed. But death makes possible the fulfillment of life. By death the man becomes an ancestor.

vi) Land of the Dead:

The dead lives in the realm or the land of the dead underground or the other side of the world. This is like the world of the human.

vii) Continuity of life: Rebirth:

The dead ancestors continue to have dealings with the living relations in the world. The dead may be reborn into the living world. This is a belief that the dead are living.

viii) Most African societies believe in a number of gods but also in one Supreme Power responsible for creating the universe and the world. There are different names for God, Nzamba along the west coast, Lezs in south centre, Mwari among the Shone, Medimo among the Lotho-Tswame, Mutunga along the east coast and Nagai among the Bantu speakers. The Supreme Being is the creator and ultimate power of the universe. There is not much of the direct worship of the Supreme Being, being too powerful. too great and too different form people to want a worship or a sacrifice.

Supreme Being holds together the web of relationship between the human beings and the environment. He is the source of the power of lower gods and human beings, living ort the dead.

***The Zulu:***

The Zulu are the single largest African ethnic group of South Africa. They are a nation speaking the Nguni language of the south Bantu linguistic family. They are concentrated in Zululand, the historical Zulu homeland now in Kwa Zulu/Natal province of South Africa. They are more than nine million in population. Traditionally, the Zulu are agriculturist, livestock rearers who keep large herds of cattle in the wooded grasslands of the Zululand. The Europeans confiscated their lands after a long period of war and conflict known in history as Zulu wars in the nineteenth century.

***Social Organisation:***

The Zulu is one of the clans of the Nguni people. In the early nineteenth century, the Nguni King Shaka combined the Nguni clans with the Zulu, and adopted the name of

Zulu as the combined name of the Nguni and Zulu for building a united nation in the Zulu empire.

The Zulu society comprises several patrilineal households, each with its rights over fields and herds under the domestic control of the senior man.

The paternal authority is so strong that the Zulu society is described as patriarchy. Polygamy is practised. The wives of a man are ranked by strict seniority under the great wife, who is the mother if the heir of the man.

The levitate, the custom of marriage of a widow to here deceased husband's brother is widely practised. The senior man of the clan, genealogically is the chief of the clan, a leader in war and a judge in peace time. As headman, he has the charge of the members of the clan.

### *Nation-wide clan system:*

A nation wide clan system under the Zulu king was adopted. All the clan chiefs were related to the king by marriage. When the Zulu empire was formed, many chiefs were married to the women of the royal line; or the royal clans men were appointed to replace the dissident chiefs. A nation wide council of the chiefs under the king was established to advise the king on administrative and judicial affairs.

### *Zulu Army:*

The Zulu was a highly organised military state. The Zulu army consisted of the boys of the adolescent age who were organised on age set. They were recruited and put in royal barracks for military raining under the control of the king. The army was divided into regiments. The soldiers were not permitted to marry without the permission of the king.

### *Zululand:*

The Zulu belonged to the Mtetwa empire built up by their king Dinginswayo (1809-17). He was succeeded by

Shaka (1816-28) who conquered the neighbouring areas and established the Zulu empire. During the reign of Dingane, the successor of Shake, the Zulu empire was penetrated by the Boers in connivance of his brother Mpande. Dingane was suppressed and Mpande became the ruler (1840-1892). However the Zulu territory was occupied by the Boers and the British who occupied Natal in 1838 and annexed it in 1843. Zululand was made a crown colony in 1887. The Zulus revolted in 1888 and the rebellion was suppressed. As a result, Zululand was annexed into Natal in 1897. And Zululand lost its political identity. In 1970's the Bantu Homeland (Kwa Zulu) was established by the apartheid government of South Africa. And in 1994, it was incorporated into Kwa Zulu/Natal province.

***The Zulu Religion:***

The Zulu religion was based on ancestor-worship and the belief in a Creator God. It was a nation or state organised religion under the control of the king. He was responsible for all the national festivals and ritual performed on behalf of the people. The rituals were performed in the worship of God on the occasion of rain making ceremony and at the time of planting season, war, drought and famine.

Zulu religion is definitely polytheism, with strong emphasis on the worship of one Supreme God.

***The Supreme God: the Lord of the Sky:***

According to Dr. Burglund, the early literatures on the Zulu religion did not indicate any Sky God or High God. But due to the pressure and challenge of Christian mission, there had developed among the traditional Zulu, an idea of the Lord of the Sky, named nKosi Ye Zulu. As explained by Dr. Booth Jr. the African religion has a belief in a Supreme Being who is the creator of the universe. Therefore, nKosi Ye Zulu of the Zulu religion, who is described as the Lord of the Sky was not an invention of the modern Zulu but the assertion of their belief in the Supreme God of their traditional faith.

The Lord of the Sky or the Supreme God is eternal. He is the source of power and might, and a source of good and evil. He is believed to be king and generous, erratic and unpredictable. People turn to him during drought and natural disaster.

### *Mode of Worship:*

It is believed that He can be approached but better be avoided except with a long preparation. Certain well known hills in Zululand are recognised as His place where no cattle graze and no people ascend. A Zulu follower says, "The prayer is offered by the rain doctor, We kneel or lie down when he speaks to the lord of the sky. When he finishes we return, without speaking. We do not talk, for the one in whose presence we are, is fretful."

### *World of Gods:*

The Zulu believes in a supernatural world of gods and deities which are described by the anthropologists, in an inaccurate term of the 'spirit world' or the world of the shades. These gods and deities, the so-called spirits play an important in the life of the Zulus. It is time of crisis, these deities brood over their descendents as a 'hen broods over her chicken'. The chief occasions are child birth, puberty, marriage, death and burial. Tit is believed that these deities supervise the transformation of the individual in different stages in life; delivery of the child into the world. Puberty makes a child into a youth; marriage makes a girl into a wife and ultimately, a mother. The Zulu diviners claim that these deities are pale .The coloured; their world is upside down; the dark stands for light, the flight for dark; the gall is as sweet as the honey. People work during day time, they are active at night. The right hand is left and the left is right. The diviners use left hand in offering to the gods.

### *Zulu Myth on Mortality of Mán:*

There is a Zulu myth of ecachtology. There is a story that, in the beginning, the Supreme God also known as Unkulunkulu instructed a chameleon to take a message to mankind saying that mankind would be immortal. Chemeleon proceeded to the human world and he was delayed due to his waywardness. Meanwhile, the Supreme God changed His mind and instructed a lizard to proceed to the world of humans with a message that mankind wold die and become mortal. Then the chameleon arrived and passed on the message of immortality for mankind. But he was too late. Mankind received the message of the lizard and did not believe the message brought by the chameleon. Thus human kind became mortal due to the waywardness of the chameleon.

### *Land of the Dead:*

The Zulus believe in the concept of the land of the dead. So the rituals connected with dead and burial are very elaborate. The dead person was buried at night so that the deceased could reach the new country at a time when he could see. The concept of the reversed world in the land of the dead exists among the beliefs of other indigenous people.

### *Zulu Ritual Dance:*

In African society including the Zulu, dance serves as a complex diversity of social purpose. Zulu dance is performed as a ritual. Of course, the Zulu war dance is famous world wide. However, the Zulu dance is the merger of the ritual and recreation. Dance is a part of Zulu religious tradition.

The Zulus are a highly developed community who have accepted Christianity but they retain their identity and are proud of the culture. That makes them look to their past wisdom and indigenous religion which is still followed by a sizeable section of the Zulu people.

## 3. THE CHEROKEE OF THE UNITED STATES:

The American Indians of the United States are the indigenous "nations" who are living in that part of the western hemisphere for the centuries. However, history, particularly, post Colombian period shows that the Amerindians were the victims of the European colonization, white man's greed for their lands, the injustice and betrayal done to them by the whitemen and their government. The American Indians who are living in the Reserves after being removed from the original habitat were reduced to a small minority of less than a million. Yet many Indian tribes (or the nations) still survive to the present times. They are now trying to assert their cultural identity despite their conversion to Christianity and acculturation with the European way of life. And the Cherokee, Creeks, Chichasaw, Choctaw, and Seninole, are a remarkable Indian tribe with a chequered history of struggle for survival. Like the other Indians, the Cherokee was also a victim of the whitemen's imperialism. They were the first people who took to the English way of life, yet no losing their identity

Professor J.W.E. Newberry writing of the growing revivalism of the native American religion made an observation on the contemporary situation. He says, "contrary to the popular belief, primal religions (traditional tribal religion) are today reviving in many parts of the world. The superior, attitude, which spread European civilization over the globe, spurred on by western Christianity and materialism, has been discredited in the twentieth century. Native faith-ways, scorned, forbidden almost destroys-reached their lowest point at the end of the nineteenth century. Their flame was extinguished.

Dr Newberry continues, "But today, the disregard for the earth for community, for spirituality, have brought the whole human enterprise into jeopardy. Arising like the phoenix from the ages, tribal people are gathering again in their ceremonial circles, remembering discarded teachings, renewing the ancient ways. As they do so, perhaps, they are laying the foundation for what they themselves are calling the "fourth nation" and a hope for a new beginning on earth." (Newberry: 1994:165).

The American Indians look to their past and tradition for guidance and inspiration. They found wisdom in their past in the long experience of their race in the tradition. It is the resurrection of the Indian wisdom, interpreted their tradition, folklore, and the folkways to the present situation. The Indian revivalism is thus the resurrection of their past wisdom.

***The Cherokee:***

The Cherokee is a remarkable and versatile community with a rich history and culture. They had accepted the American democratic rule, adopted the European technology and were converted to Christianity. But they failed to get recognition and protection of their homeland, their values and traditions form the whitemen. They suffered greatly in the past. At the end of the twentieth century they are reviving their cultural tradition.

The Cherokee are a tribe of the Iroquoian linguistic and ethnic group. They inhabited the eastern Tennessee, western Oklahomo and western North Carolina. In the past, they settled around the Great Lakes in the north and migrated to the south after defeat at the hands of the Delaware and Iroquoian tribes. They lived in Georgia and Caroliona in the Appalachian mountains. In 1650, the population of the Cherokee was estimated to be around 22,000 occupying a territory of 40, 000 sq. miles.

The life and culture of the Cherokee had some similarity with the Creek and other Indians of south east United States. The Cherokee describes themselves as a nation (though we are using the term, tribe). The Cherokee 'nation' was continued of a loose social confederacy of red (war) and white (peace) towns. Town is the biggest territorial unit for their social organisation. The town is like and organised village. The chiefs of the red towns are subordinated to the supreme war chief; and the chiefs of the peace towns provided sanctuary for the wrongdoers and the war ceremonies at the occasion of battle or raid were conducted by the red towns.

***Township:***

The Cherokee town was an economic, social and political organisation under a patriarchal chief. There were seven "mother towns" which were the headquarters of the seven clans to which the Cherokee are divided. Each headquarter served as the capital of the towns of the surrounding areas. Over the whole tribe are officials at the headquarter of important town, but the central authority is weak. The Cherokee are egalitarian and so do not have a strong political organisation.

Every Cherokee town was well fortified with a wooden pallisade. At the centre of the town "were the public buildings, set in terrace in the more important town. There was a 'square' formed four shed like structure where they are performed the sacred communal ceremonies tin the centre. Man sat in council, seated according to rank, to decide the matter of war and peace, and hunting, to settle the disputes among the villagers. Just of f the square, there was a tall building, the hot house, where the villages met for business and recreation during the inclement weather. The individual dwelling houses were located on the streets, stretching out form the public centre. The

Cherokee houses were window with bark with one dooor and smoke hole on the roof. A town had 30-60 houses.

The agricultural farms were cultivated in the fields around the towns. The private gardens were worked by the womenfolk. During the planting and harvesting, the whole community worked together. Each family contributed grains to the common public greenery under the supervision of the chief.

The Cherokee were a warlike tribe. They were in constant warfare with the neighbouring tribes. Glory of victory in war was the supreme idea of a Cherokee youth. Personal excellence in war was highly commended in society. In the 18tyh century, during ht American War of Independence, the Cherokee took the side of the British crown. After the American independence, there continued a constant warfare between the Cherokee and the United States. President George Washington, the first American President and his secretary of State, Henry Knox made several treaties in 1784 and 1791. According to the second Treaty which was signed in a council with the forty Cherokee chiefs the following provisions were agreed upon.

i) The boundary between the Cherokee country and the territory of the United States was defined.

ii) The United Sates guaranteed the Cherokee nation against further encroachments on their territory by the whitemen.

iii) The treaty assured the Cherokee to have a "greater degree of civilization, to be the herders of cattles and cultivators of agricultural crops instead of being hunters.

***Era of Peace and Progress:***

The first decades of the $19^{th}$ century was an era of peace and progress. Despite the irritating conflicts on the border as the whitemen tried to encroach of the Cherokee lands, the Cherokee decided to develop their land and their way of life. They adopted the European technology in agriculture, by the use of the plough, animal husbandry, horticulture and cotton plantation. The Cherokee tried to assimilate with the culture of the whitemen. They formed a government with a constitution modeled after that of the United States under the leadership of a liberal Chief Juna Laski, But this friendly relation between the Cherokee and the United States government was disliked by a rash frontier man, named Andrew Jackson of Tennessee who attacked the American government. However, the Cherokee made friendship with Andrew Jackson in his war against the Creeks which was regretted by the Cherokee as a mistake. The Cherokee continued their assimilation with the white American. They adopted the English mode of farming, weaving and house building. They took up education very seriously. One Cherokee genius named Sequoyah invented the Cherokee syllabary according to which system books in Cherokee were written and printed. In a very short period, the Cherokee became widely educated. Even a newspaper in Cherokee, the first tribal language newspaper of the United States, the Cherokee Phoenix was published in 1828. Religious literature, translations from the Christians scriptures were published through Cherokee syllabary.

### *The Removal of the Cherokee from Georgia:*

Andrew Jackson of Tennessee opposed the Cherokee in the Congress, as they were provided some protection by the Treaty sanctioned by President Washington. Jackson represented the vested interests of the land hungry and greedy American President in 1828, he consistently followed an anti-Indian policy of removing the Indian tribes to the unhabited west. He passed the Indian Removal Act in 1830. It coincided with the discovery of gold in the Cherokee land of Georgia. He instigated the state of Georgia to adopt a similar state Removal Act to evacuate the Cherokee from the gold rich land in Georgia. The Cherokee under the leadership and filed a case in the Supreme Court of the United States which was a historic landmark, Cherokee Nation vs State of Georgia. The Supreme Court under the Chief Justice John Marshall ruled in favour of the Cherokee who were declared to be a distinct nation having a treaty relation with the United States. But President Jackson and the George State refused to implement the order of the Supreme Court. The whitemen induced schism among the Cherokee leadership; the minority supported Treaty of New Echote (1835) was forcibly signed. According to this treaty, the Cherokee land east of the Mississippi river was sold for only five million dollar. The Cherokees were evicted from their homeland under the Removal Act of 1830. Seven thousand U.S. army gathered 15,000 Cherokees in camps. Their holdings were plundered and confiscated by the white residents. They were sent away in groups of one thousand men, women and children.

### *The Trail of Tears (1838-39):*

The forcible evacuation of the helpless Cherokee under their Chief John Ross with an inhuman treatment of the American army is known in American (Cherokee) history as Trail of Tears. It was a great tragedy; 4000 Cherokee died in the 116-day journey of tears, suffering, sickness, and death. They were settled at the north eastern Oklahoma. Some Cherokee escaped the Trail to the western North Carolina where they lived ever since. There were other removed tribes like the Creek, Chickasaw, Choctaw and Seminale. Oklahoma grew into an Indian majority state in 1907. But through the intervention of several commissions, the lands of the Indians were alienated from them and taken over by the whitemen. By 1906, all the traditional governments of the Indians including the Cherokee were abolished. In the late 20th century, the Cherokee population in Oklahoma reached 47,000 and in western North Carolina about 4000, total being about 50,000 souls.

***The Cherokee Social System:***

The Cherokee did not possess an elaborate social organisation. Their way of life was aimed at fostering individual self reliance. The Cherokee society was organised in band which was a loosely organised collection of people occupying a particular tract of land. Several bands were organised into a tribe which was a social unit rather than a political unit. The Cherokee tribe was a group of people who spoke a common language and followed a common custom. Unlike the other Indians, the social stratification was weak in the Cherokee society: chiefs, other clan chiefs and common peoples.

***Chiefship:***

The Cherokee clan is a sub unit of the tribe. The clan loyalty is very string, both during war and peace time. Clan is the important kin group in the region where agriculture is more important vocation. Members of a clan heave a clan obligation towards one another like clan duty and clan hospitality.

The marriages in traditional Cherokee society are unstable. The marriage system is not elaborate. Marriage was conducted with the symbolic exchange of gifts between the groom and the bride. Divorce was frequent. Polygamy was permitted.

The naming of a child is an exclusive monopoly of a clan. There are accepted names of a clan which are related with some animals or spirits. Every child is named after one of the totem names used by the clan. Totem literally means relations. There are Young, wolf, Hawk, Deer, Heron, etc. the totem has a special relation with the clan.

### *Cherokee Religion, belief in the one great spirit:*

The Cherokee like other Indian tribes believes in a Supreme Being or the Master of Breath. He is described as the one Great Spirit. The whole supernatural world is represented by the Spiritual power of the Great Spirit who is named in Iraquoian word, Orenda. The Great Spirit or the Supreme Being is the creator of the universe, the sun, the moon, the earth and fire. And according to Dr. Newberry the American thought and action are governed by symbolism. The Great Spirit is symbolized by a circle which is basic in nature, the shape of the sun and moon wheeling stars, rotating seasons, action of birds and animals. Everything tries to be round. The form is evident in everything they do-in myth, ceremony, art and community organisation. Essential to the circle is its centre. From this is created. This is the symbol of the Great Spirit (*see jacket cover of the book*).

### *The Myth of Creation:*

According to the creation myth in the beginning, there was nothing; a big flood (a primal deluge) occurred. The supernatural beings from the sky plunged to secure a portion of mud caused by the deluge. That portion of the earth mud was expanded into earth island. Thus was created the earth. There was a cosmic struggle between the good spirits and evil spirits. The good ones bestowed boon on the man kind and the evil one was the source of death and misfortune.

The world was viewed as divided into four quarters of four cardinal directions presided over by a deity. The structure is represented by the symbol of four.

Four is the sacred number. Four stands for the four quarters of the earth, the four seasons colours of the universe which are mode of elements, earth, air, water and fire.

### Spirit World and Spirit Power:

It is believed that the world was populated by the deities and spirits of natural objects, like the sun, the moon, thunder, fire, etc. these spirits have spirit power, which transcends the spirit world. They believe in the supernatural power- a force in the universe. This spirit power like the Polynesian Mana is equivalent with the Orenda of the Iroquoian (Cherokee).

The delicate man-nature relationship is well expressed through the Cherokee religion and world view. The world is perceived as animated by ghosts, witches and spirits which are essence of plants, natural objects and phenomenon.

### Soul:

Soul is endowed to man and animal. Animal has been given some reverence. It was believed that slain animals would seek vengeance on the hunter through their supernatural chiefs. Thus hunting has become a sacred act, with tabu, ritual and sacrifices.

The plant world was considered friendly to mankind. The Cherokee gives a great importance to nature, plant world and herbal medicine. They believe that any animal disease could be cured by a plant antidote.

The religious festivals were connected with agriculture and crops. The Cherokee festival of the Green Corn or the Busk was performed in honour of the maize. The festivals infused annual renewal of the fertility and sacred fire was enkindled: old debts and grudges were forgotten and a sense of commands was regenerated.

### Dream, Vision and Priest:

The Cherokee had a well developed priesthood. The priests were given training to become full time practitioners of rites and rituals. They were responsible for the spiritual health of the community. They performed the collective religious rituals for the annual festivals. The priests preformed the ritual on any occassion, both secular and spiritual.

The medicine men and the shaman priests interpret the dreams and vision of the common men. According to the belief, dream indicate the cause of illness, the curing power of the individual and the means of maintaining good fortune. The dreams were given so much importance that dreams could influence the decision of the family and the community during council meetings. However, reliance on dreams did not mean living in fantasy. According to Cherokee ethos, self reliance and individual competence are the factors of success in life. The magico-medical practitioners looked after the disease and sickness.

***Land of the dead:***

The Cherokee believed that when a man died the resting place of the dead was in the land of the setting sun in the western direction or in the celestial firmament. The souls of the dead were believed to hover around the relatives or the community to persuade them in their journey to eternity. There are two concepts of the resting place of the dead; in the land of the setting sun which is perhaps, the land of the dead and the celestial firmament in the sly may be the abode of God of heaven.

There was an elaborate death ceremony performed to ward off the influence of the soul of the dead by giving them an honourable farewell and to protect the living from the evil influence.

Death was not considered a natural event. The cause of the death was ascribed to the malevolent animal spirit or witched or the machination of the sorcerers. If a death was caused by a human agent, vengeance must be taken. The Cherokee, as noted above depended on the plants and herbal medicine to cure the illness.

The Cherokee is widely use music, both vocal and instrumental in the invocation to the One Great Spirit, in the worship of the sun, the moon, the earth and other elements of nature, water, air and winds. The Cherokee is promoting the preservation and development of their culture, the music craft, folklore, and fold dance. They are showing the way for the revival and substance of their indigenous religious belief.

Lastly, the study of the primordial religion of the American Indian through symbolism made by Dr. J.W.E. Newberry has raised the philosophical foundation of which every sensible follower of the indigenous belief will be grateful everywhere.

**4. SINKYO OF KOREA:**

Korea has seen the coming of Confucianism, Buddhism and Christianity in her sling history. But behind the "outward imposition of foreign faiths, is the traditional religion of Korea known as Sinkyo which has been called a religion without a name. (Harrie Conn: 1994: 145).

According to Sinkyo philosophy there are five magnetic aspects of this religion. Man and cosmos, man and cosmic norms, man and his destiny and man and his salvation.

The world is a religious arena, a cosmos inhabited by gods of the heaven, the earth, water and trees. Humanity is in rhythm with such a world, and the forces of nature control life and death, fertility and become personified and god like.

***Creation:***

According to the Korean creation myth, Tagun was the legendary founder of Korea. Ung, a son of heaven converted a bear into a female. The bear transformed woman could not get any husband to marry her. Ung also changed his form and married her. A son was born and named Tagun. Tagun, the son of the heavenly parents founded Korea. And every Korean must conform to this cosmic form.

According to the Sinkyo faith, mankind and nature meet in harmony of the opposites. The opposites complement each other. They are represented by the great forces of Yin and Yang. Harvier Lann thinks that 'Yin' represents the "being" and Yang represents the "non being".

The Yin is negative, passive, weak and destructive. The Yang is positive, active, strong, and constructive. Out of their intervention which is cosmic dialectic, harmony is achieved and recreated again and again. The Yin is female, mother, soft and dark. The Yang is male, father, strong, hard and bright. The Yin and Yang represent the independent female and male forces of life, the independent female and male forces of life represented by the symbols of divided circle with two sides, white and black. The harmony of the cosmic working of Yin and Yang and the harmony of fire elements, wood, metal, fire, water and earth must be maintained (*see the symbol of Sankyo on the jacket cover of the book*).

However, the cosmic harmony is often broken; man desires to have salvation from the world. The Sinkyo has to meet the craving of man for salvation. Man performs rituals and ceremonies to harmonise the force of nature and the activities of mankind. To quote Conn again, "When the rice paddles are ploughed in the field, a farmer's band pacifies the spirits of the earth with music and ritual, when the ridge pole of a new house is raised wine and food are thrown at it while members of the household chant hymns for good luck, long life and many sons."

They perform the ritual and sacrifice which is the way back to the paradise lost. Interpretation/Propitiation of the spirits was performed to satisfy the spirits. They perform the ceremonies during the burial of the dead to satisfy the earth spirit.

The shaman or the diviner, called the Mudang was employed to cure the physical and mental disease. The Mudang is engaged to perform a communal sacrifice for good crops during harvest, for fisherman for safe journey and good catch, for fertility of barren woman, recall the spirit of the dead and lead him to the kingdom of the blessed (heaven).

The Sinkyo came into contact with the foreign religions. The Confucian emphasis on filial deity strengthened the ancestor-worship.

***Supreme being:***

Of all the gods, the heavenly god, Hananim or Hanunum was the highest, the Supreme God. He brings sunlight and rain, lightning; drought and disaster are given as punishment. By His favour, the mankind lives. At the time of national disaster, the king prayed to the Heavenly Father by confessing his sins and those of his people.

Sinkyo made adjustment with Confucianism, Buddhism and even with Christianity. And Sinkyo tradition lives on.

## CHAPTER THREE

# INDIGENOUS FAITHS REFORM MOVEMENTS IN NORTH EAST INDIA

A renaissance is sweeping across the indigenous people of India's north east; it is a movement for the revitalization of the indigenous faith and culture. There is a realization among the elite and the religious leaders to preserve their identity and culture. They feel the need to organise their religion to meet the onslaught on their religion and culture made by the Christian missionary movements. They are also greatly encouraged and emboldened by the national policy of secularism and protection of the cultural heritage of the country. They are aware of the global efforts to preserve and propagate the religion and philosophy of the indigenous people as expressed by the United Nations' Draft Declaration of the Rights of the Indigenous Peoples.

### NATURE OF THE REVITALIZATION MOVEMENT:

We may highlight the nature of the movement.

i) The phenomenon of reform and revitalization is an introspective response to meet the threat and the challenge of the alien religion, particularly Christianity towards the indigenous culture, religion and identity.

ii) The revitalization is carried out by the establishment of the community or tribal level religious authorities to organise the religion which was traditionally organised by the village level authority and functionaries.

iii) The indigenous religions which do not have traditional names are given a name with a well explained theology and philosophy. The nameless religions have become name specific religions with a distinct identity.

iv) The tribal religion believes in the existence and worship of a Supreme God. The revitalized religions have turned towards monotheism, though traditionally they are polytheistic. Obnoxious religious taboos and practices are either abolished or reformed. They give emphasis to the salvation of the soul after death. The soul are believed to have gone to the land of the dead and to Heaven. They do not go to hell or lake of fire as propounded by Christianity. Their cod eof social and moral conduct will make the follower of an indigenous man, a bearer of truth and righteousness.

v) They believe in the continuous communion between God and men. So they strengthen the traditional channel of communication between God and man.

vi) The leadership of the movement comes from the highly educated elite of the community who use culture and literature as their instrument of propagation.

vii) They seek and get the international or national level recognition as a distinct religion form organisations, like the International Association for Religious Freedom, Oxford and the United Religion Initiative, San Francisco.

## THE BRITISH CONQUEST AND THE CHRISTIANITY:

The British conquest of north east India in the 19th century heralded the advent of the Christian missions and the conversion of the tribes into Christianity like the Garo, the Khasi, the Naga, the Kuki, the Mizo and others. The Christian missionaries condemned the indigenous religion and culture. They described the tribe as savage, devil worshipper, heathen, pagan, worshippers of wild spirits and animist. Both the ethrographers and the missionaries were influenced by E.B. Tylor and adopted his term "Animism" to mean the tribal religion in official and academic publication. Now many anthropologists and indigenous leaders have rejected the term "Animism" and new nomenclatures like Primal religion, Primeval religion and Primordial religions have been used.

While many indigenous communities were converted into the Christianity, the followers of the indigenous faiths started the movement for reforms or revitalization. During the colonial period, there were several religious reformers, namely U Jeebon Roy of the Khasis, Jadonang and Rani Gaidinliu for the Zeliangrong Naga, Naoria Phullo was a Meitei thinker who tried to revitalize the Meitei Sanamahi religion. Among the Bodos of Assam, Gurudev Kalicharan Brahma was a remarkable religious reformer who introduced the Brahma Dharma. Recently, it was Talom Rukbo, an Adi scholar of Arunachal Pradesh who organised the traditional faith, Donyi-Polo.

There are religious traditions like Rangfraism among the Tangsas of Changlang district of Arunachal Pradesh, Nunna Lalchhunga Kua (Family of Living God) among the Mizo and Bathowism among the Bodos, the Lhikeri among the Chakhesang Naga. We take up three movements in the present sturdy, the Seng Khasi, the Zeliangrong Religious Movement (including Heraka cult) and the Donyi-Polo.

## 1. SENG KHASI MOVEMENT:

In the later parts of the 19th century, there were a number of Khasi leaders and thinkers who made an effort for the "reawakening of respect and regard for their own culture after the advent of the British" among the Khasi Christian converts. (H.K. Synrem: 1982:45) the prominent leaders were U Rabon Sing Kharsuk (-1910) who wrote on the Khasi religion and rituals, and U Hommunai Diengdoh who edited the first Khasi monthly, U Khasi Myna (The Khasi Today) in 1895 and wrote extensively on the Khasi religion and also pointing out the weakness an shortcomings of the Bible. He was an ex-Christian convert.

The most prominent Khasi leader was U Jeebon Roy who cherished a vision of a glorious Khasi race. He was regarded as the "apostle of Khasi renaissance" which led to the establishment of the Seng Khasi (the Khasi organisation, community or the Meeting of the community and clans). He was the spirit behind the historic movement.

### *Babu Jeebon Roy (1838-1903)*

Babu Jeebon Roy was born at Saitsohpen, Sohra (Cherrapunji) of the present state of Meghalaya in 1838. His father, U Ram Singh was a prominent trader. Jeebon Roy was sent by Rev. Alexander Lish to study at Serampore Mission in Bengal, but he did not complete his education beyond the primary level. He joined the service of the East India Company in 1858 as a clerk in the office of the Principal Assistant Commissioner at Cherrapunji. During the Jaintia Rebellion of 1862, he served as a writer and interpreter to General Showers. He was promoted to Sub-Inspector of Police. In 1877, Jeebon Roy was appointed as the Extra-Assistant Commissioner (EAC) when Col. H.S. Bivar was appointed the Deputy Commissioner of the Khasi and Jaintia Hills. At the time, the British government entrusted the Calvinist Welsh Mission to run all the schools with the books written in the Roman script to enable the Khasi Christian converts to read the Bible. Realizing the importance of western education, he established a private High School. His son Sibcharan Roy passed the Entrance Examination (Matriculation) from the School which was ultimately taken over by the government.

Jeebon Roy wrote several books in Khasi on the themes like, the Ramayana, Hithpadesha, Budha Chartia, Chaitanya Charita and a Khasi translation of Bhagavat Gita. After retirement, he took to livestock farming, horticulture farming and trading in limestone and coal mines.

Jeebon Roy was aware that the traditional faith and culture of the Khasis were being obliterated by the Christian Missionaries, by converting them into Christianity. He wrote books on Khasi religion. In 1897, his Ka Niam Jong Ki Khasi (The Khasi Religion) was published. He gave a warning in this book as reproduced by Ms Synrem, "The people will completely forget their religion and culture with the coming of the Christian Mission, the Roman Catholic Mission, the Unitarian Mission, the Brahmo Mission; The poor religion of the Khasis without any written record will pass into oblivion and we will one day forget completely." In 1900, he wrote "Ka Kitab ba Batai Pynshynni Shphang Uwei U Blie (A Book on One God) in which he pleaded for the universality of God in Khasi religion and monotheism. He died in 1903. He was the foremost social worker and reformer of Khasi–Jaintia society.

### *Foundation of the Seng Khasi, 1899*

When the Seng Khasi was being established, Jeebon Roy donated a plot of land at Mawkha in Shillong, for the organisation. The Seng Khasi was founded on 23, November, 1899 with U Rashmohan Roy Nongrum as the Chairman and Babu Chandranath Roy Dkhar as Secretary. The threat to the Khasi cultural identity led ultimately to the establishment of the Seng Khasi. There were several prominent Khasi personalities who were the founding leaders of this organsiation. The Seng Khasi was greatly helped by U Sibcharan Roy (1862-1952), the son of U Jeebon Roy, though he was not a member of the organisation. He published two papers, U Nongpira (The Watchman, 1903) and U Nongpynrin (the Deliverer, 1930). He delivered public lectures on Khasi religion. He published these lectures in "Ka Niam Ki Khasi, Ka Niam Tip Blei Tip Briew" (The Khasi Religion, Man Knowing and God Knowing Religion).

## *Essence of Khasi Religion*

After intensive study by the learned scholars and leaders the Khasi religion came to be properly understood both by Khasi themselves and the outside people. H. Onderson Mawrie in his "Essence of Khasi Religion" writes of the Khasi conception of God and the relation between God and man which is the basis of the religion. Mawrie writes, "U Blei, the name we gave to God is He and only. He is the creator and sustainer of the Universe. He is almighty and all powerful, omniscient and omnipresent. Being all in all, He is above Gender and we can call Him, 'U Blei' or 'Ka Blei'. He is also above number we can call Him, 'U Blei', 'Ka Blei'. Being to be-all and end-all, we give him different names in different spheres of our life and different aspects of His creation, Our Khasi religion is monotheistic and these names connote attributing the absoluteness of God in the Universe."

The name of the Khasi religion was popularly named Niam Khasi. Niam means religion. It is a combination of two words. 'Nia' which means 'reason' and 'Im' meaning 'living'. So Niam means "Living Reason" (R.T. Rymbai). Khasi religion goes by the name of Ka Niam Tipbrew Ka Niam Ti Blei (Man Knowing and God Knowing Religion) (Mawrie). The Seng Khasi bases its tenets mainly on the writing of U Jeebon Roy, U Sibcharan Roy, U Homurai

Deingdoh and U Ras Mohon Roy. The recent competent scholars are H.O. Mawrei, R.T. Rymbai and U Hipson Roy.

***Aims and objectives of the Seng Khasi***

The Seng Khasi has the following objectives:

i) To foster a sense of brother hood among the Khasis who still retain then socio-cultural and religious heritage.

ii) To revive the true faith of the forefathers.

iii) To understand the true meaning of consciousness and truth as handed down through generations which are being neglected, misled and blinded by the teachings of foreigners.

iv) To create consciousness about U Blei who always resides in the heart of a devotee and therefore, the devotee need not be imported or borrowed from outside.

v) To earn righteousness through service and respect for one another's fellowmen with a sense of humanity strictly in accordance with the precept of Kur and Kha (kinship).

vi) To work for the mental and physical development of fellow members and to regulate the way of living both morally and socially.

vii) To work for the advancement of education.

viii) To encourage national sports like archery, cultural dances and social festivals.

ix) To undertake welfare and development activities such as maintenance of cremation grounds for those who dispose off the dead according to Khasi tradition and custom (Synrem and U Hipson Roy).

There is another organization named Ka Seng Ki Nongshat Nongkhein to revive the Khasi religion. They do the same works as the Seng Khasi does. Their aim is to bring peace and righteousness to the individual, the family, the clan, the society and the state as a whole by reviving once again the communication with U Blei (God) through rituals with the help of signs and symbols, U Blei gave to U Briew (man).

Due to the efforts of the enlightened leaders especially U Hipson Roy, H. Onderson Mawrei and R.T. Rymbai the Seng Khasi has been granted recognition as a distinct religion by the International Association for Religious Freedom.

## 2. THE ZELIANGRONG RELIGIOUS MOVEMENT:

The Zeliangrong movement under the leadership of Haipou Jadonang and Rani Gaidinliu was a comprehensive social movement. It was a reaction against the British colonial rule. It aimed at the liberation from the colonial rule, social integration of all cognate tribes of the Zeliangrong Naga covering the "Zeme, Liangmei and Rongmei" and religious reforms and cultural resurgence. Apart from the political objective of a Naga Raj, the social and religious reforms are of far reaching consequences. The revitalization of the Zeliangrong religion and culture was the main theme of the movement. The colonial authorities looked at this movement as a rebellion against the British and the Christians looked at it as an anti Christian heather movement. The reform movement was definitely not against the Christians or Christianity. The Christian constituted a microscopic minority in the Zeliangrong population in the late 1920's. The leader of the movement was Haipou Jadonang.

### *Jadonang (1950-1931):*

Jadonang was born in 1905 at the small village of Kambiron in Manipur state in the present district of

Tamenglong. He had an extraordinary childhood. He grew up as a mystic healer and diviner. He was inspired and advised through dream divination by God Bisnu of Bhuban hills of Cachar in Assam to carry out religious and social activities. He went on pilgrimage to the holy caves of God Bisnu to seek advice and inspiration form him. As per divine revelation, Jadonang announced the abolition of many evil social and religious practices. He constructed temples for TingKao Ragwang or Tingwang, the Supreme God and installed the images of God. He became very popular as a healer, diviner and religious leader. He was regarded as the Messiah deliverer, for whom the Zeliangrong people had been waiting, who would liberate the people from the life of sufferings and bondage. He composed hymns and ritual dances for the worship of the TingKao Rangwang. His last pilgrimage to Bhuban hills was in January, 1931. On return, he was arrested by the British government for proclaiming a "Naga Raj" and executed on 29, August, 1931.

## RELIGIOUS LEGACY OF JADONANG:

The religious legacy of Jadonang was his religious reforms in the traditional and orthodox Zeliangrong religious and conservative society. His reforms were a synthesis of monotheism with idolatory and temple culture, simplified and rationalized form of religious worship leading towards social solidarity among the Zeliangrong people reviving the common past and origin.

Jadonang's contribution was the emphasis on the worship of the Supreme God, TingKao Ragwang (or Tingwang) in rational form, community and individual worship of God for welfare and prosperity. The worship consists of prayer, ritual dances, ritual hymns and sacrifices. He insisted on an individual devotion and prayer to TingKao Ragwang with folded hands. His abolition of the taboos and gennas had purified the traditional religion without deviating from the essence of the Zeliangrong religion. He composed hymns and ritual dances as revealed by God. His two temples showed some outward influence of church architecture and Hindu idolatory. There are two trends in his legacy; one is sporadic and unorganized link with the traditional religion, the other is the innovative and organised form of a reformed cult which was, after thirty years, named Heraka by his follower and disciple, the legendary freedom fighter, Rani Gaidinliu. In their last pilgrimage to the holy cave of God Bisnu, TingKao Ragwang revealed a set of religious beliefs and practices which formed the essence of the Heraka cult.

### *Rani Gaidinliu (1915-1903):*

After the martydom of Jadonang, the leadership of the Zeliangrong movement, both military and religious was taken up by Gaidinliu who put her master's ideology into practice. Gaidinliu was born on 26, January, 1905 in the village of Nung Kao in Manipur state. She was an independent and strong willed girl of character and sincerity, deeply religious and ambitious. She was associated with her master's movement at a young age of 13 years. With her spiritual commitment, organisational skill, talent of music, Gaidinliu emerged as the natural lieutenant of Jadonang. In the pilgrimage to Bhuban hills in January, 1931, she was blessed to be the leader of her people and the prophet of the reformed religion revealed to her and Haipou Jadonang by Supreme God, Ting Kao Ragwang. Gaidinliu firmly believed that she had the divine sanction to the revolt against the British and fight for the independence. After the execution of Jadonang, Gaidinliu organised the rebellion from April, 1931 to October, 1932. During the period, she was in the centre-stage of military campaign and religious activities. The British attempt to arrest her and suppress her revolt made her a legendary figure. She was ultimately arrested in October, 1932 from the Zeme village of Pulomi (Poilwa) in Naga Hills, and was sentenced to life imprisonment by the Political Agent in Manipur state.

The martydom of Jadonang and imprisonment of Gaidinliu did not put an end to the Zeliangrong uprising. Several leaders of the Zeme and Liangmei of the Naga Hills of Assam and Manipur state continued the movement. The Manipur state government won over many of the leaders of the Rongmei section of the Zeliangrong people Rani Gaidinliu who was eulogized buy Pandit Jawaharlal Nehru as the 'Rani' of the Nagas in 1937, was released after 14 years of imprisonment. But she was kept in the isolated Chang village of Yimrap in Tuensang upto 1951. She was allowed to return to her native state of Manipur, and her district, Tamenglong. She continued her social and religious activities. In 1960, she had a difference of opinion with the underground Naga rebels, both political and religious. She went underground again with an army of four hundred soldiers to defend her religion and political rights. During the period 1960-66 she organised her religion into 'Heraka cult'. She became the patron-saint of the Heraka religion which was ultimately organised into the Zeliangrong Heraka Association, covering the Zeliangrong areas of the state of Nagaland, Assam and Manipur. Rani Gaidinliu passed away in 17, February, 1993 at her native village of Nung Kao in Manipur.

## THE HERAKA RELIGION: BELIEF IN TINGWANG

Heraka literally means "Pure". And the Heraka religion is the pure or reformed religion of the Zeliangrong people, which according to Rani Gaidinliu is the essence of the Zeliangrong belief as revealed by TingKao Ragwang or Tingwang.

The Heraka believes in Tingwang, the cause or the Root of all creation, the Creator of the Universe, Tingwang is the Dispenser of all boons, benevolent and good to all good-doers. He is worshipped by all. The belief in the worship of one Supreme God as practised by Heraka is a concept of monotheism. The traditional Zelaingrong religion as explained is polytheistic as these is a system of worship of pantheon of gods.

The Heraka does not worship smaller gods and goddess of the Zeliangrong pantheon; sacrifices to these gods are abolished. There is no worship of the village presiding deities or the worship of ancestors.

The mode of worship is in the form of prayer at the individual or community congregation singing the hymns in the praise of Tingwang. They worship in congregation on every full moon day known as Bupu-Ngai (Festival of the Full moon). They offer sacrifices to Tingwang and partake the feast in the name of Tingwang. All sacrifices were abolished. They offer prayer at sunrise and sunset. Rani Gaidinliu composed appropriate hymns on such occassions. They perform the ritual dances. Heraka had simplified all the rites of birth, marriage and death. They also abolished all genna collectively and individually. They perform the traditional festivals, but in a very simplified form. The Association organised annual conferences and festivals for women and youth.

## THE ZELIANGRONG HERAKA ASSOCIATION

The Zeliangrong Heraka Association is the supreme authority of the Heraka religion. It is organized at the village level through the office of Peipou. Rani Gaidinliu was the patron-saint of the Heraka when she was alive. The Association had attracted a large number of educated young men and young women to its fold. The president of the Association is a former Christian theologian, a close associate of Rani Gaidinliu, a greater orator and effective organizer named N.C. Zeliang of Nagaland. He is assisted by several leaders, the most prominent is Ram Kui Newme of Haflong in North Cachar Hills. The Heraka Association has women and youth wings. They published the teachings of Heraka and Rani Gaidinliu, both in English and Zeme. They organized conferences and festivals to which the dignitaries of other faiths were frequently invited. Due to the great influence of N.C., Zeliang and RamKui Newme, the Heraka is well known throughout India. They have also exerted influence on the followers of the indigenous Naga faiths in Nagaland to orgainse onto religious authorities.

## EMERGENCE OF TING KAO RAGWANG CHAP RAIK (TRC):

A legacy of Jadonang is the practice of the religious pilgrimage to the holy caves of God Bisnu in the Bhuban hills. It is believed that God Bisnu used to communicate through the holy priests (Mhu) and diviner on the religious practices. With the instructions from God Bisnu, the followers of the traditional faith started making annual congregations and pilgrimage to the holy caves. A temple of God Bisnu was constructed. Every sensible member of the Zeliangrong community who follows the traditional faith felt the threat to this religion and culture form the alien religion.

## FORMATION OF THE ZELIANGRONG RELIGIOUS COUNCIL, 1994:

In March, 1993, a meeting of the Zeliangrong community leaders of the states of Manipur, Assam and Nagaland was held at Bhuban hill to discuss the status and future of the Zeliangrong religion. They constituted a steering committee which visited all the villages in three states. After one year of intensive mass contact, they organised the first conference on the Zeliangrong religion at Imphal on 14-16, April, 1994. The conference after three days of deliberation resolved to establish the Zeliangrong Religious Council (Zeliangrong Ra Chapriak Phom) to act as the sole authority of the Zeliangrong religion and organise it in a democratic way. They adopted a constitution and elected the office bearers. The conference also declared the name of the Zeliangrong Indigenous religion to be christened as "TingKao Ragwang Chapriak", the religion of the TingKao Ragwang, the Supreme God and it was announced at the ceremony of Laogai Karikmei (Holding the Iron Hoe in the name of God).

The Zeliangrong Religious Council had mobilized the Zeliangrong villages. They published several religious books especially the authoritative "Ringlon and Theilon". Rites in respect of Birth, Marriage and Death, three prayer and Hymnal books. They constructed an impressive House of Worship of Ting Kao Ragwang at Chingmeirong, Imphal. They declared the full moon day as the prayer day of Ting Kao Ragwang. They declared the abolition of the taboo (Nuhmei) on the occassion of the unnatural death. They adopted the Cosmos (universe) as the symbol (Boudan) of Ting Kao Ragwang. The council has two wings, known as the executive council and the ecclesiastical council.

They organised prayer and ceremonies and singing of hymns on the full moon day and on every Sunday. On these prayer days, these is religious congregation in which a large number of people, men, women and girls including children including the followers of other faiths including foreigners participated. The council also had organised singing classes in the villages. The women wing, the Mathenmei-Phon has been quite active. They attend marriage, death ceremonies and festivals and sing the hymns, they have a youth wing also, Chabon Phom.

The Council had also enrolled the TingKao Ragwang Chapriak as a member of the United Religion Initiative based at San Francisco through the cooperation circle of Manipur State. They have also participated in many inter-religious assemblies and conferences in India.

The Heraka and the TingKao Ragwang Chapriak popularly known by its abbreviation, TRC are two complementary religious traditions, the first is monotheistic and the second in polytheistic with strong emphasis on the Supreme God (TingKao Ragwang as the single God Head). Both Tingwang of the Heraka and TingKao Ragwang of the TRC are one and the same Divinity. The TRC maintains the traditional system but abolished all unnecessary taboos and gennas like the Heraka. Both have appeared as refined and rational theology and philosophy.

## 3. DONYI-POLO MOVEMENT:

The Donyi-Polo of Arunachal Pradesh is a remarkable indigenous renaissance. Donyi-Polo has been a traditional belief of the Adi and Tani group of tribes. Worship of the sun and the moon is a universal form of worship in many parts of the world. But in course of time, the dual worship of Donyi, the sun and Polo, the moon had become institutionalised in Arunachal Pradesh.

### *Dr. Verrier Elwin on Donyi-Polo*

Dr. Verrier Elwin, the well known anthropologist and the former Advisor in North Eastern Frontier Agency (NEFA) refers to Donyi-Polo in his A Philosophy for NEFA in 1957. He writes, "There is a general belief in a Supreme God who is just, benevolent and good. For example, Donyi-Pollo (Donyi-Polo) the sun-moon god of all the Adi groups is regarded as the great witness in the sky, the upholder of truth."

He further comments, "Although the angust being does not seem to have created the world, the reigns supreme sun challenged in the heavens; he is the eye of the world; he is as important to man as the eye to the body. He watches everything; he is the witness of truth, he shows the men to go the way to go, he protects them, he treats them with mercy. Above all, he is the lord of the truth and an oath taken on his name is the most binding of all. He is the unifying force behind the popular religion from Siang to upper Kamla." (Elwin; 1957: 210-11)

### *Talom Rukbo and Donyi-Polo*

Talom Rukbo (1938-2001) was the father figure of the Donyi-Polo movement. He was the leader and philosopher of the Donyi-Polo faith. Rukbo was born on 1st, December 1938. He belonged to the Adi community. He was educated at Pashighat and Shillong in school and college. After his education, he entered the NEFA Administration in 1960. During the Chinese invasion in 1962, Talom Rukbo joined the SSB (Service, Security Bureau) to organise the people into the village volunteer force to defend against the invaders. Later on, he became the Language Officer of the Administration and was posted at Pashighat, In this capacity he took up the initiative to study, the language, literature, folklore and religion of the Adis. He was also made the Secretary of the Adi Cultural and Literary Society at Pashighat. He published several tracts on Adi folklore, religion and culture. He used to tour the villages with a group of performing artists. During these visits, he explained to the masses about the threat faced by the Adi culture and religion from the alien religions, and exhorted them to pressure their religion and culture.

Talom Rukbo wrote, "With the advent of colonization the British entered our Paradise (Arunachal Pradesh) and introduced into our midst the most dangerous and crafty unit of militancy-the church. The church, Christian missionaries quickly capitalized on the innocence of our forefathers. They fraudulently convinced our people that we were barbarous, and converted some into Christianity. Having put into them the fear of God, the temptation of the Paradise, they put the Bible into their hand and employed the local youth to translate it and hymns into their local dialects. The book, was made for free distribution in the local areas. Those brain washed youth became their tools and hand made for propagation of their religion and erected churches to attract the innocent Arunachal people, thus converting them ingot missionaries. The so-called "services" they offered in form of medicine and schools were thin disguises for their crooked purpose of conversion. They declared that the converted person must discard i) animist practices, ii) our festivals and that our Gods and Goddesses were Satan (evil spirits-Satan). Christians must depend only on the cross for their safety and security. Slowly this created frequent disturbances and social disharmony. The Christian missionaries were stooping to the lowest, most uncivilized means to tear the social fabric of our society apart." (Rukbo, The truth Every Bharatiya should Know, Guwahati, 2002).

Talom Rukbo's ceaseless efforts created a stir in the minds of the people. The Adis flocked to the cultural festivals organised by him. There were serious rethinking and introspection among the educated youth of the Adi community on the critical situation.

### *Formation of Donyi-Polo Yelam Kebang, 1986*

According to Kaalang Borang, an associate of Talom Rukbo, "serious thinking was dome and ultimately the thrust of the movement for cultural revivalism was shifted towards religion and a touch of spirituality was given to the efforts of the Society. Thus an organisation under the name or title of Donyi-Polo Yelam Kebang was formed on 31, December, 1986 under the guidance of Talom Rukbo, the Secretary of the Adi Cultural and Literary Society". Donyi-Polo was already a very widespread religious cult in Arunachal Pradesh. Talom Rukbo organised the traditional Donyi-Polo as a functional religion. Under the Kebang, Donyi-Polo had emerged as a well formulated and well oragnised religion.

### *Objectives of Donyi Polo Yelam Kebang*

i) The main purpose of the Kebang (body) was to organise the Donyi-Polo as a functional religion under the authority of the Kebang. The Yelam Kebang is the authority of the Donyi Polo faith.

ii) To make the idols of Donyi Polo and other benevolent gods and to construct temples.

iii) To publish books of hymns and prayer , the traditional teachings and injunctions of the Donyi Polo known as Aabang (Shastras)

iv) To establish prayer centres known as Gangging which are constructed to accommodate people for prayer and worship.

v) To celebrate the festivals which are the ingredients of the faith,

vi) To preserve and follow the age-old traditions as the basis of any innovation, modification and reform in the religious practice.

## THE ESSENCE OF DONYI-POLO

The Kebang published the Aabangs which are described as the Shastras of the Donyi Polo which provide the philosophy and theology of the cult. The Aabangs give directives to the devotees. It provides the texts in Adi and English on the concept of Donyi Poloism, the Kebang published an authoritative treatise and text on the Donyi Polo religion. It is titles: "Donyi Poloism: A Religion", in 1997, probably written by Talom Rukbo himself. It was the English version of the Adi text.

"Donyi Polo is the supreme power of the universe. The supreme power is omnipotent, omniscient and omnipresent. The supreme power is formless, felt but unseen. The Sun (Donyi) and the moon (Polo) are regarded as the visible physical representation of the supreme power, Hence Donyi-Polo. According to Aabangs of the Donyi-Polo, the universe was created out of Keyum which means nothingness.

According to the Aabang, Donyi-Polo in its spiritual manifestation, means God Himself. Donyi-Polo in its physical form means the Sun and the moon. And Donyi-Polo in its philosophical interpretation means faith. The spiritual and philosophical doctrines of Donyi-Polo according to their treatise, are as follows:

i) It is the supreme governing power of the universe.

ii) It is the ever probing power.

iii) It is the supreme Judge of the highest court of eternal law.

iv) It is the source of life and energy of the living beings.

v) It is the Divine light, wisdom, knowledge, truth and brotherhood.

Th Donyi-Polo Yelam Kebang gives a strong emphasis on mediation and prayers for which the hymns were composed and circulated. They conducted the sermon on the teachings of Donyi-Polo on every Saturday. They organised orientation courses twice a year on the Donyi Polo philosophy.

The Donyi Polo Yelam Kebang has tried to expand the canvass of the Donyi Polo over the kindred tribes of neighbouring area. In order to cover the Tani group of tribes namely Mishing, Nyishi, Apa Tani, Galxxong and the Adi, the Donyi Polo Spiritual Society of Arunachal Pradesh was constituted. The Donyi Polo was recognised as a distinct religion by the International Association for Religious Freedom, Oxford. Talom Rukbo attended the conferences organised by IARF in Europe and Asia. It was mostly due to his efforts with a strong backing from educated people that Donyi Polo had arrived at its present glorious position.

Dr. Hamlet Barch, a historian of repute observed on the philosophy and theology of the Donyi Polo as follows:

"The traditional divinal belief of the Adis is based upon the plural manifestation of the divinity. The adoption of Donyi Polo as the Supreme Deity is the shift of ideology of faith of plural manifestation to the dual manifestation. The compound divinity of Donyi Polo represents the theological condensation of the polytheist onto a dual divinity."

He further writes, "The Donyi Polo has emerged as a symbol of sympathetic force. It represents the Almighty in His Omnipotent, Omniscient and Omnipresent forms. Donyi Polo is the source of light, the generator of life and sole protector of all creatures. It is Donyi Polo which provides the essence of truth, justice and beauty, morality, love and goodness." It is the greatest tribute to Donyi Polo faith.

## CHAPTER FOUR

# THE PRIMORDIAL RELIGION: A CASE STUDY OF THE ZELIANGRONG RELIGION

The Zelaingrong Nagas of Manipur, Assam and Nagaland are an ancient tribal community who are divided into three cognate groups. Zeme, Liangmai and Rongmei who have a common ethnic and linguistic origin, a common past, a common social and cultural pattern and religious belief. They are Tibeto-Burmans of the southern Mongoloid. Linguistically they belong to the Naga-Bodo sub-family of the Tibeto-Burman with dialectical variations. They have a long history and a well developed religion. The religion is a traditional indigenous religion, a clear case of a primordial religion which was historically evolved and based on various customs and tradition from the many past. The religion has no founder but there were a number of law givers, prophets and diviners who made revelations of God's message to man and society. Essentially, the Zeliangrong religion is a polytheism, there is an element of Henotheism as there is a belief and worship of one Supreme God out of many gods.

### THEOLOGY OF ZELIANGRONG RELIGION

Theology is a field of study, thought and analysis that treats of God, His Attributes and His relation to the universe and man. And religion is a set of beliefs concerning the cause, nature and purpose of the universe, especially considered on the creation of a super human agency, usually involving devotional and ritual observances, and often having a moral code for the conduct of human affairs. In simple language, religion is a system of worship of God by man, and a code of social and moral conduct for the people following the particular religion. The religion of the Zeliangrong has the usual features of a primordial religion and it is definitely not animism.

## ONE SUPREME GOD

The Zeliangrong people believe in the eternal existence of one Supreme God has no beginning. He is the creator of the universe, gods, men and all living beings. He is the regulator of the universe, giver and source of life, dispenser of plenty and justice. No body except Him can give life. He is named Ting Kao Ragwang (the Universal God or the King of the gods of the Universe and Heaven). He is also called Tingwang (Lord of the Heaven). He is the Sky God and High God. He is believed to be Omnipresent, Omniscient and Omnipotent.

## PATTERN OF GODS AND DEITIES

Zeliangrong religion is a stated above polytheism, belief in multiple gods. There is a belief in the pantheon of Gods, below the Supreme God. Pantheism is a feature of Zeliangrong theology. The pantheon consists of gods on earth. These gods are below the Supreme God. Ting Kao Ragwang asked a god named Didampu to rule the world of the humans, the lower realm. Didampu retired as Bunglawang, the God of the earthquake. His nephew born of his sister was made the rule of the lower realm. He was named Ragwang (king of gods). The pantheon therefore consists of Ragwang and seven brothers who are divinities, lords of nature and village presiding deities. Every community and tribe have always passed through a stage of social and religious development in which they worship the supernatural beings along with the Supreme Bring as the creator.

The Zeliangrong people passed through the different stages of their mental and spiritual horizon relating to their religious beliefs and practices. The Zeliangrong religion, though essentially polytheistic in nature, has a strong monotheistic element as found in the worship of the Supreme God in a philosophical form, Ting Kao Ragwang.

## WORSHIP OF NATURE

There is a belief that some elements of nature have been endowed with divine power and status, like the fire, water, the wind and the earth. These elements are worshipped in the form of lords or kings of fire, water, wind and the earth. Recently, the reformed Heraka cult has started the worship of the Sun. There is no worship of stone or boulder, trees of forests or mountain peaks as alleged by ill-informed writers and observers. There is a belief that gods of these places are worshipped as "presiding deity."

## THE PRESIDING DEITIES OF THE VILLAGE

As the traditional Zeliangrong society is organised at the village level the world view of the people is limited to the villages. They worship the deities presiding over their villages. These deities are guardian-protectors of the villages who are to be worshipped or sometime propitiated. They are generally described as the Shong or Bambu and each village has a specific name of the deity.

## ANCESTOR-WORSHIP

There is the concept of the eternity and permanence of the soul of man which can be created with the power of Ting Kao Ragwang. There is the belief in the birth, rebirth and incarnation of human soul. The human soul does not die. The souls of the ancestors are not separated from the family-they remain as protectors of the particular household, family or lineage. They are worshipped by the concerned family. The ancestors are, in general known as the Kairao. Ancestor worship which appears to be more a form of honouring the living dead is a strong feature of the Zelaingrong religion. Offerings are made to the spirits of the ancestors almost everyday, at every ritual or religious ceremony and during the festival. There is a set of rituals for the worship of the ancestors.

## FORMS OF WORSHIP

There are community and individual forms of the worship of God and deities. While prayers are usually chanted, sacrifice and offering accompanied by the ritual hymns are the main form of the worship of the God and deities of the Zeliangrong pantheon. The form of worship ranges from a small offering of water, grass, leaves to the great sacrifices of Maku-Ballu and Taraang. The worship of Supreme God, Ting Kao Ragwang is through prayer and sacrifice, based on the concept of worship and charity to the community. The people pray to God with folded hands and by kneeling down.

## RITES AND CEREMONIES

Rites and ceremonies are performed to worship the Supreme God, the gods of the Lower Realm (earth) and specific deities.

i) The great sacrifices of Balu and Taraang and other smaller ceremonies are offered to Ting Kao Ragwang for salvation of soul and for going to Heaven after death.

ii) Ting Kao Ragwang Kalummei is the worship of the Supreme God.

iii) Raren Loumei is the worship of all the gods of the Zeliangrong pantheon including Ragwang and his seven brother-gods.

The rituals involving the offering of sacrifices to all gods are performed by the village community or the individuals. The gods who are offered sacrifices and worship constitute the pantheon which comprise Ragwang and his seven brother gods, the gods of the natural elements, deities presiding the villages and places.

1. Ragwang and his Seven Brothers: Ragwang Na-Ren Chanei)

    i) Ragwang, king of gods of the Lower Realm (Na-Ragwang), his abode is at Mt. Koubru.

    ii) Bisnu (Munshnu, Manchanu, Bonchanu, Buisnu). His abode is in the holy caves of Bhuban hills, Cachar).

    iii) Napsinmei (Laorang) His abode is in Napsinmei Mountain peak of Luwanglon Khullen, Old Cachar Road)

    iv) Kara-Ngong, his abode is at Puching (Khebuching).

    v) Koklou, his abode is Pongringlong in Koubru mountain.

    vi) Chonchai, his abode is at Kasokbut in Taosang village.

    vii) Chara Kilongmei, his abode is in Bena, Thonglang, I.T. Road.

    viii) Dimei

    (It may be noted that the names of these gods differ from region to region)

2. Deities Representing Nature:
   i) Pon Gwang: God of the wind
   ii) Mai Gwang: God of Fire
   iii) Di: Earth

## KAIRAO-KALUMMEI

The worship of the ancestor is performed by the individual families.

### *Worship of Other Deities:*

i) Ran Kaomei: (Calling or worship of Wealth)

ii) Nap Kaomei: (Calling of worship of Goddess of Paddy)

iii) Bu-Kaomei: (Calling of the Soul)

iv) Dampa Khonmei: (Calling of the Goddess of creation, Dampa pui)

## PROPITIATION OF SPIRITS

There is a practice of the propitiation of spirits not to disturb humans. This is called Ra Khaangmei. This is different from the worship of God, which is known as Ra-Kalummei.

## CONCEPT OF GOD

The philosophical foundation of the Zeliangrong religion is based on the cosmic view, moral and social values, and attitude towards God, man, life and death which were evolved through the ages. At the philosophical level, Ting Kao Ragwang is the supreme God of the Universe, who is the creator and protector of the whole universe. He is the creator of man, gods, living beings, the sun, the moon and other natural objects. He is eternal and ageless, no beginning and no end. He is All-knowing, All powerful, and

All-present; prayer and chanting is the form of worship of Ting Kao Ragwang. While sacrifices, big and small are offered to Him, approach to Him is more spiritual than sacrifices, ritual dance, hymns ands songs are offered to Him. He is described as Pasumeipu-Padammeipu, creator and ordainer, Businmeipu, giver of Soul.

The regulation of the universe and human world is supervised by the gods of the lower Realm at the wish of Ting Kao Ragwang, the gods of the pantheon have more connection with man. It appears that ht worship of these gods was started at a later period of the pre-historic time where the Zeliangrong people settled down in their habitat in the western hills of Manipur, southern Nagaland and eastern Cachar and north Cachar Hills. The gods of the pantheon are regarded as the benefactors and protectors of man. It is also believed that there exists a world of gods or deities who decide on the life and death, fortune and destiny of man.

## THE CONCEPT OF SOUL

According to the creation myth, Ting Kao Ragwang commanded Dampapu and Dampapui, two deities to create men. They created man and woman in the image of Ting Kao Ragwang. They were life less and soul less. They requested Ting Kao Ragwang for life and soul of the humans. Ting Kao Ragwang breathed life and soul into the bodies made of clay. Only Ting Kao Ragwang could give life.

There is a belief that soul, though ordained by God is a part of the human person, There is also a belief in the eternity of the soul of man, birth and rebirth of man. Soul does not die, only the body abandoned by soul is regarded as dead. They have the practice of Bu Kaomei, calling of soul implying that the soul exists outside the human body yet resides in it.

## LIFE AFTER DEATH

The human soul after the physical death of the man will go to the land of the dead, Taroi-Lam. He will lead another life in that world. He will live among his ancestors who are supposed to have another life of their own. The soul of man may be reborn in the human world. There is a god ruling over the land of the Dead, known as Taroi Gwang, (king of the Taroi-Lam). The funeral ceremonies give a vivid picture of the passage of the dead form the world of the living to the land of the dead. There is also belief that the human soul in the land of the dead may get punishment from the king of the land of the dead.

## CONCEPT OF HEAVEN

The Supreme God, Ting Kao Rapwang is believed to be living in His Heaven, the abode of Ting Kao Ragwang. It is commonly believed that the good doers and the performer of the big sacrifices to God will go to Heaven after their death. Every Zeliangrong man or woman aims to go to Heaven after death to live a life of salvation. There is also a belief in the existence of Ragwang Kai, the house of the God of lower realm, where the dream diviners (Mangkeimei) and other seers go in their dram to negotiate with god for the welfare of man for whom they are pleading. Ting Kao Ragwang Kai, the Heaven is the ultimate aim of a man's life. However, there is a difference between the abode of the Supreme God and the land of the deal. Men go to Land of dead: he may be reborn to the human world. Going to Heaven to live with Ting Kao Ragwang is great spiritual journey, full of many difficulties to be overcome.

## NO HELL

There is no concept of hell in Zeliangrong religion in the Judaistic-Christian theological sense. But the king of the Land of the dead will punish the evil doers of the human world when they come to his land. Hell is alien to the Zeliangrong philosophy of life.

## CONCEPT OF SIN

Sin is a deviation from the accepted social, moral and spiritual norm of a society. Sin, in the Zeliangrong belief, is committed when a man breaks or villages the social and moral code of conduct. He gets divine punishment in different forms. In this life or in the world after death, including the transformation of ht human soul into lower beings of insects, plants and vegetable and ultimately extinction of life and conversion into inanimate objects. However, there is the belief in the atonement of sin or wrong doing of men by God, if appropriate worship and prayer are offered to Him.

## CODE OF SOCIAL AND MORAL CONDUCT

The Zeliangrong religion is a code of social and moral conduct which is enforced and accepted by the people.

## NEIHMEI

Man's collective worship of God is performed with the observation of the Neihmei which is the collective abstention from work and worship for a particular day or period. There are various Neihmei which are described by the anthropologists as genna, originated from Angami word, Kenna. The Neihmei is observed by the community as well as by the individual families. The Zeliangrong religious practice was once overburdened with numerous Neihmei which were rather unnecessary. It was the root cause of orthodoxy and superstition in Zeliangrong society, Haipou Jadonang, a religious reformer in the early twentieth century abolished many genna which were concurred subsequently by the community organisation.

## NUH-MEI

Customs relating to the performance of the rites of passage, like birth and birth ceremonies, marriage, death and death ceremonies cannot be violated. It is a taboo. This prohibition is called Nuh-mei. Those who break the Nuhmei are condemned as the violators of the social and moral code. The religious practices are enforced through this taboo, known as the Nuhmei.

## MORALITY

The Zeliangrong moral ethos and concept of morality are the reflection of their world view of life, death, heroic deed, defence of the village performance of religious sacrifice, performance of his duty as a member of his dormitory and the village council known as the Pei. The moral sense of the Zeliangrong community is quite strong. Righteousness, sense of justice, loyalty to God, his dormitory and Village Community are regarded the supreme duty of a Zelaingrong man.

## THE RELIGIOUS ORGANISATION

The Zeliangrong religion is organised through the village council called Pei consisting of the elders and priests, who manage both the secular and religious affairs of the village. The village Pei is the religious authority. And it operates through the various social institutions like the dormitories of the youth and girls (Khangchu and Luchu), the organisation of married women (Mathenmei), the old women forum (Kangjapui) and the House of Elders (Ganchang Kaibang).

## THE PRIESTHOOD

The village elders take the help to the chief priest of the village, known as the Tingku and the priests who are known as Mhus for the performance 0of the various religious rites and the festivals. The Mhus act as the medium between gods and men. Some of the spiritual priests are seers and little prophets whose advice is necessary to sustain the Zeliangrong religion. God reveals His message and directives to man through these Mhus. The Mhus are dream diviners. They are the shaman priests and priestesses. Shamanism is an aspect of the Zeliangrong religious practice.

## THE FESTIVALS

The Zeliangrong festivals are performed at the various stages of the agricultural operation and seasons according to the lunar calendar. The Zeliangrong festivals and religion are closely linked up with their agricultural occupation. There are no uniform dates except the months in which the various festival are performed. These festivals are the rejoicings of the community, expressed through prayer to God for His blessings for welfare and plenty. The cultural values, the aesthetic sense and creativity of the Zeliangrong people are expressed through the festivals. The Zeliangrong religion is sustained by their colourful festivals. The ritual dances and music are also a form of worship of God.

## EVOLUTION OF AN ORGANISED RELIGION

The traditional religion as shown above is organised at the village level. It has no community religious organisation at the tribe level. There are basic similarity in the concept and practice of Zeliangrong religious belief and practice though there are local or regional variations. The priests and priestesses, the Mhus and the dream diviners and visionaries have provided the necessary divine revelations which maintain the connection between man and God. With the coming of the British rule, the head hunting, the main cause of inter village feuds was prohibited. And the community social organisations also stopped such inhuman practices. It was Haipou Jadonang, who first organised the religion into a functional body. Haipou Jadonang was a religious mystic, a social reformer and a political rebel. It was further developed by his disciple, Rani Gaidinliu, the legendary freedom fighter and religious head into the Hera Cult. The Champa society was also founded on the monotheistic cult of worshipping the single Supreme God, Ting Kao Ragwang. Both Heraka and Champa are inclined towards a philosophical monotheism.

The pilgrimage to the hole cave of Haipou Bisnu in Bhaban hills in Cachar where a shrine is constructed and dedicated to Haipou Bismu led to several religious cogregations of the Zeliangrong people of Assam, Manipur and Nagaland. The holy prehistoric natural cave and the shrine of Haipou Bismu have become a centre of religious activities under the leadership of some enlightened and learned leaders. People had felt the need of All Zeliangrong Religious Authority.

## THE QUESTION OF A COMMON NAME

The issue of a commonly accepted name of Zeliangrong religion was another issue which engaged the attention of the religious leaders. There were serious queries made by the educated youth about the accepted name of the religion. The traditional religion is generally named after the name of the tribe. It is also named after the name of the God they worship.

## THE ZELIANGRONG RELIGIOUS COUNCIL: TING KAO RAGWANG CHAP RIAK

Every religion has a God, a mode of worship, a name and an organisation to organise, promote and regulate the functioning of a particular religion. In a great religious conference, held on 14-15, April, 1994 at Imphal, the Zeliangrong Religious Council was established to constitute the authority of the Zeliangrong religion. The name of the Zeliangrong religion was christened after the name of the

Supreme God, Ting Kao Ragwang. It was ritually declared that the Zeliangrong religion was named as Ting Kao Ragwang Chap Riak (TRC).

The Zeliangrong Religious Council has organised the Ting Kao Ragwang ChapRiak (TRC) in a democratic and proper way. After a lot of research, they published a book on the rites of passage, called Ringlon and Theilon (Zeliangrong Rites of Passage), religious hymns have been published and circulated in cassettes. The council had abolished all taboo in the unnatural death. They declared every full moon day and every Sunday as prayer day.

The Government of Manipur, on the request of the Zeliangrong Religious Council have declared the Gaan Ngai, the greatest of the Zeliangrong festival as a state holiday.

The Council had constructed an impressive House of Worship of TingoKao Ragwang at Imphal.

Thus, the formation of the Zeliangong Religious Council and christening of the TingKao Ragwang ChapRiak are landmarks in the religious history of the Zeliangrong people.

# APPENDIX

# THE NAMES OF THE INDIGENOUS RELIGIOUS AND CULTURAL ORGANISATIONS OF THE NORTH EAST INDIA

1. The North East Janajati Religion and Culture Protection Forum is the common platform of all the native organisations of the north east region to work collectively. The Forum was formed at Guwahati at a meeting on 1-2, April, 2002.

**ASSAM**

2. All Bathou Religious Union (ABRU), an organisation of the Bodo-Kachari of Assam.
3. The Brahma Samaj, an organisation of the Bodo-Kacharis who believe in Nirankar Brahma and perform yagya for the blessing of God. They stop animal sacrifice. It was founded by Gurudev Kalicharan Brahma.
4. All Assam Koch-Raj Bangshi Sammilon.
5. Hemphu Mukrang Aman, a religious organisation of the Karbis of Assam which works for the

preservation, protection and progress of the Karbi primordial religion.

6. Lakhiman Sangh – a religious organisation of the Karbis founded by Guru Safa Ram Dili who follow Vaisnavism, blended with traditional Karbi traditions.
7. Shiva Narayan Hemphu Aman – an organisation founded by a Sanyasin. The followers consist of the immigrants from Chatisgarh, Adivasi, Bengali and Karbis.
8. All Assam Munda Mahasabha.
9. All Dimasa Mass Prayer.
10. Zeliangrong Heraka. Association (North Cachar Hill)

**ARUNACHAL PRADESH**

11. The Indigenous Faith and Culture Society of Arunachal Pradesh, an apex organisation of the tribal communities of the state.
12. The Donyi-Polo Yelam Kebang, Pashighat.
13. Nishi Indigenous Faith and Culture Society of Arunachal Pradesh.
14. Idu (Mishmi) Cultural and Literary Society.
15. Adi Cultural and Literary Society.
16. Galong Welfare Society.
17. Donyi Polo Nyedar Namlo Cultural Council.
18. Rangfraa Faith Promotion Society.
19. Cultural and Literary Society of Mishmi.
20. Apa Tani Gora Association.
21. Nokte Welfare Society.
22. All Arunachal Pradesh Priests Association.

## MEGHALAYA

23. Seng Khasi, Founded in 1898 at Shillong.
24. Seng Raj, The socio-religious organisation of the Jaintia community.
25. Ka-Seng (United Endeavour Society), Coordination Community of the Seng Khasi and Seng Raj.
26. Seng Khih Long, Another body of the Khasi which organizes Lumpung (religious assembly) of the Khasi and Jaintia Ka Sengba Nongshod Nongkhein Hynnietotrep Hynniew Skum.
27. Niamtrey, an organisation of the Khasi Priests.
28. Santan satsang Samiti, a religious body of the Hindu Hajong.

## NAGALAND

29. The Zeliangrong Heraka Association, started by Hai Pou Jadonang and practised by Rani Gaidinliu, formally organised by N.C. Zeliang on 5 January, 1974 operaters in Nagaland, Assam and Manipur.
30. Zeliangrong Pou Pei Cheng, another organisation of the Zeliangrong Nagas who fellow primordial religion.
31. Japfii Phiki Pfutsana Keseko Kehou, an Angami Naga religious organisation for primordial religion.
32. Chakhesang Lhikiri Lenyii Kezumi Mapou, a religious organisation of the Chakhesang Nagas.
33. Pochuri Lani Nale Kaveri, an organisation of the Pochuri Nagas
34. Dimasa Dharma Sabha of (Assam and Negaland).

**MANIPUR**

35. The Zeliangrong Religious Council, Assam, Manipur and Nagaland, Office Chingmeirong, Imphal.
36. Poumai Zenat Association, Liyai, Senapati District.

**MIZORAM**

37. Nunna Lal Chunkia a religious organisation of the Mizos working for the preservation and revival of primordial religion of the Mizos.

**TRIPURA**

38. Jamatia Hoda, a very old religious and social organisation of the Jamatia community of Tripura.
39. Baba Garia Mission.
40. Mag Cultural Welfare Society.
41. Malsom Dafa (an organisation of Malsom community)
42. Tripuri Chunlai Buthok (an organisation of the Lipuni)

**SIKKIM**

43. Sikkim Lepcha Association.
44. Sikkim Lepcha Bhutia Apexx Committee.
45. Himalaya Budhist Association, There may be several organisation other the above listed organisations.

**Source:** 1. Shri Jagdamba Mall, Convener, North East India Janajati Religion and Culture Protection Forum.

2. A Rousing Call from the North East, Dharmaraj, Heritage Foundation, Guwahati, 2004.

# BIBLIOGRAPHY


## CHAPTER ONE

1. E.B. Tylor, Animism in William A. Lena and Evon Z. Voget (Ed.), Reader in Comparative Religion, 1987, (4th Edn.).
2. J. Troisi, Tribal Religion, Religious Beliefs and Reactions of the Santals, New Delhi, 1979.
3. Martin D. Stringer, Rethinking Animism, Thoughts from the infancy of our Discipline, Journal of Royal Anthropological Institute London, 1994.
4. Sujata Miri (Ed.) Religion and Society of North East India. New Delhi, 1980.
5. Harold Turner, World of the Spirits in Primal Religions in World Religions published by Lion Publishing Oxford, 1994.
6. Ivar Lissner, Man. God and Magic (Transtated from German) London, 1961.

## CHAPTER TWO

7. Rev. James Irwin, Case Studies on Primal Religion: The Maoris of New Zealand Lion Handbook World Religion. 1994, Oxford.
8. Dr. Axel-Ivar Berglund, Primal Religion: Case Studies of the Zulu in World Religion Oxford. 1994.
9. Harvei M. Conn, Primel Religion: Korea in world Religions, 1994. Oxford.

10. J.W.E. Newberry, Primal Religion: Native North American, World Religion, Oxford. 1994.

11. Newell S. Booth Jr. Primal Religion: The Afican Religion in World Religion. 1994, Oxford.

12. Angie Debo, A History of the Indians of the United States 1993, Oklahoma.

**CHAPTER THREE**

13. H.K. Synrem, Revivalism in Khasi Society 1992. Delhi.

14. Hamlet Barch, The History and Culture of Khasi 1967, Shillong.

15. U. Hipson Roy, The Khasi Heritage, 1969, Shillong.

16. H. Onderson Mawrie, the Essence of the Khasi Religion. Published by U. Hipson Roy IFAS (Retd.), 1981, Shillong.

17. R.T. Rymbai, Some Aspects of the Religion of the Khasi-Pnar in S. Miri (Ed.) Society and Religion in North East India, 1980. Delhi.

18. Mang Kasong Khongsei, His Vision and Mission (Life History of U Jeebon Roy) in the Heritage Eplorer, December, 2003. Guwahati.

19. Maurie Dale Shah, Facets of Khasi Culture in North East Treasure, 2004, Guwahati.

20. Saradha Kharbangar, The True Tenets of the Khasi Religion in Treasure North East, 2004 Guwahati.

21. Gangmumei Kamei, Jadonang, A Mystic Naga Rebel, 2002 (2nd Edn). Imphal.

22. Lanbilung Gonmei, Movement of the Zeliangrong Religion towards Philosophical and Theological Refinement, in Van Bandhu, October, 2002, New Delhi.

23. N.C. Zeliang, Herakamei Leu 1974, Kohima.

24. Gangmumei Kamei. Concept of Heraka Religion in Kerakame Leu, 1974, Kohima.
25. The Religious Conception of Naga Ranima Gaidinliu by Heraka Women Society, Nagaland in Heritage Explorer February, 2001 Guwahati.
26. Verrier Elwin. A Philosophy for NEFA 1957, Shillong.
27. Donyi PoloYelam Kebang, Donyi Poloism, A Religion, Pashighat.
28. Hamlet Barch, Encyclopedia of the North East Vol. I Arunachal Pradesh.
29. Talom Rukbo, The Truth Every Bharatiya should know, Heritage Explorer, December, 2002, Guwahati.
30. Kaaling Barang, Preservation and Promotion of the Faith and Culture of North East, Treasury North East 2004. Guwahati.

**CHAPTER FOUR**

31. Chaoba Kamson (Ed.) Commemorative Volume on the Conference on Zeliangrong Religion Imphal, 1994.
32. Souvenir of the Zeliangrong Religious Council, Inauguration of the Tingkao Rapwang Kalumkai, Imphal, May, 6, 2001.
33. R. Marulung, Kashoi Khatni Kadam (in Rongmei), 1988. Imphal.
34. R. Marutung, Naga Dharma Amasung Houna Lonchar, (in Manipuri) 1983. Imphal.
35. Ringlon – Theilon (Rites of Passage) published by Zeliangrong Religious Council, Impha, 1988.
36. Gangmumei Kamei, The Ting Kao Ragwang Chapriak: The Zaliangrong Primordial Religion, Published by the Zaliangrong Religious Council, 2005, Imphal.

# INDEX